Always Change a Winning Team

Always Change a Winning Team

*Why Reinvention and Change
are Prerequisites for Business Success*

Peter P. Robertson

Copyright © 2005 Scriptum, Schiedam

First published in Dutch as *Ontsnappen uit S-catraz* by
Scriptum Publishers, Schiedam, 2003
Translator: Jonathan Ellis

This translation first published in 2005 by Marshall Cavendish Business
An imprint of Marshall Cavendish (Asia) Private Limited
A member of Times Publishing Limited
Times Centre, 1 New Industrial Road
Singapore 536196
T: +65 6213 9288
F: +65 6285 4871
E: te@sg.marshallcavendish.com
Online bookstore: www.marshallcavendish.com/genref

This book is published by special arrangement with
Cyan Communications Limited
4.3 The Ziggurat
60–66 Saffron Hill
London EC1N 8QX
www.cyanbooks.com

A CIP record for this book is available from the British Library

ISBN 981 261 800 7 (Asia & ANZ)
ISBN 0-9542829-9-X (Rest of world)

Designed and typeset by Cambridge Publishing Management

Printed and bound in Great Britain by TJ International Ltd, Padstow, Cornwall

Contents

Introduction

We are right in the middle of an exceptionally important process that will once again put this company firmly on the map as an e-commerce company with a magnificent soul.
Carly Fiorina, former president and CEO of Hewlett-Packard[1]

THIS book investigates the boundaries within which people in organizations are prepared to explore and change, and the implications for management. It is all about a choice that you make yourself. If you are convinced that leadership based on values and trust can and should go hand in hand with financial and social profit, then you will find many things here that will help you further develop and implement such a vision. If you are of a different opinion, you will find little here that tries to convince you to change your mind.

The Russian author Fyodor Dostoevsky (1821–1881) is reported to have said that somebody should not write a book until they have tried everything possible to prevent it being written. This is another in a long line of books that attempts to make a contribution to the leadership and management of an organization that, because of information technology, is suddenly faced with rapid acceleration. Why have I not prevented this book being written?

Largely because others have convinced me that virtually nothing has yet been written about applying concepts from ethology to the management of organizations. That is strange to say the least. You will have to decide for yourself whether I should have prevented the publication of this book.

Ethology is also known as *comparative behavioral studies*. This science has been around for more than 100 years and, after World War II, received widespread recognition thanks to Nobel Prize winners such as Konrad Lorenz, Nikolaas Tinbergen, and Karl von Frisch. My own definition of *ethology* is that it is "the science that, using the perspective of evolution, investigates how and why a specific behavior develops and what drives that behavior." The society in which we live today has, from an evolutionary perspective, only been around for a very short time and differs markedly from the world of many million years ago in which our behavior originated.

Our genetic make-up takes much longer to change than our society. Much of our behavior can be better understood if we try to discover the logic of it viewed from the situation in which it has, over many million years, made a contribution to the development of the human species. When we look at things from this perspective, ethology can provide some extremely interesting insights that bring unexpected depth to the management of organizations.

There is a wide range of literature devoted to ethology; anybody doing a search on the Internet using the term *ethology* or the related term *sociobiology* will find more than enough information. Much of the information, however, concerns the animal kingdom and gives details that few managers will need to know for their jobs. I have restricted myself to general literature, and mainly to literature that translates ethology to the human situation.[2]

Within ethology, concepts have been developed that deal with how people form human bonds (*attachment*) and how people are attracted to the unknown (*exploration*). Organizations derive their internal strength from a combination of teamwork, loyalty, and the courage to undergo constant change. Using the concepts of attachment and exploration, they can understand the emotional intelligence that is required for constant change. For this reason, it is strange that so little has been written about applying ethology to organizations. And so – after yet another abortive search on the Internet – I decided not to prevent the writing of this book.

Nevertheless, the interest in ethology is growing. A number of leading dot.com booksellers have recently added several titles catalogued under *attachment* or *ethology* to their selections. The interest has also been picked up by the press, as is shown in a long article by M. Talbot that appeared a few years ago in the *New York Times*.[3] There is also a gradual interest being shown by business. The *Harvard Business Review* recently published an article entitled "How hardwired is human behavior?"[4] about evolutionary psychology; it includes, for the first time, the word *attachment* used in its ethological sense.

I sometimes think that the lack of interest in ethology may be due to the fact that, some 100 years ago, Sigmund Freud refused to accept the concept of evolution. Even though Freud said that Darwin's concept of evolution had stimulated him to study medicine, he remained, until his death in 1939, a disciple of the French zoologist Jean-Baptiste de Lamarck (1744–1829); the latter's theory – long since discredited and only of historical interest – said that the characteristics developed by a living organism during its life are passed on to its descendants.[5] Many of the social behavioral directions that emerged in psychology during the last century arose from, or were connected to, the psychoanalytical approach laid down by Freud. Perhaps this is one reason why there was less of an appetite for implementing concepts from evolution in this area than in, for example, the fields of biology or biochemistry. I believe managers should be slightly concerned about this, since the behavioral scientific input into areas such as human resources – recruitment, diagnosis, selection, assessment, and training of staff – is based, directly or indirectly, on a psychology that still partly lacks any input from the study of evolution. Managers should ask themselves whether the behavioral tools they use are "state of the art."

The British psychiatrist John Bowlby (1907–1990) is one of the few to have tried – in his heroic trilogy *Attachment and Loss*[6] – to integrate ethology into human psychology. In this trilogy, Bowlby not only shows how ethological concepts can fundamentally contribute to an explanation of human behavior, but also how they fundamentally differ from behavioral and psychoanalytical concepts. I cannot avoid the impression that the establishment did not look favorably on all this. The cool reception given to his work in the established psychoanalytic circles may possibly explain why ethology has taken such a long time to reach the field of organizational management.

As I said above, this book investigates the boundaries within which people in organizations are prepared to explore and change. I have not approached this investigation from one single perspective. During my many years of study, I have also strayed into other areas such as cybernetics, information science, chaos and complexity theory, and neurophysiology. Yet despite all these varying perspectives, one has always remained central: ethology. It is impossible to imagine that any single person could even begin to master all those branches of science that I mentioned. But I am certain of two things. First, that many of the things I suggest are simplifications, and second, that they often do not give a full idea of the current state of affairs and may even, on occasion, not be completely correct. Nevertheless, simplification is essential when trying to create a synthesis. While I was writing this book, many people encouraged me to stress the applicability of the model and to accept any imperfections for what they are.

All this, however, does not imply that I have simply written the first thing that came into my head. My ideas and explanations are based on facts, but, in the choice of those facts and the way in which I intuitively simplify and combine them, I have allowed myself to adopt a very personal view. Even if the model that is constructed in this book proves to be untenable and if I am attacked for overplaying my hand, I would still expect the model to – or rather, I am convinced the model will – contribute to a new view of people, organizations, and change processes.

Ethologists will quite possibly not be pleased with the choices made in this book to define terms. This book is not written for them, though. Instead, it is written for the uninitiated in the field of ethology, such as managers and leaders of organizations. An example to explain what I mean: *Set goal*, a term used by Bowlby in his description of the attachment system, is used in this book to mean "focus of security and attachment." I do not want to be superficial, but nor do I want to fall into the trap of using inflated language and fashionable terms that litter so many management books; I hope the choices I have made in terminology are useful.

Some of those who read the first concepts for this book warned me not to compare too frequently the relationships in an organization with those between a child and its parents. That, they said, could backfire and give the book an undesirably pedagogic character. I have done my best to listen to them and have tried to avoid any "damaging exaggeration" in the text. On the other hand, managers have repeatedly told me how they use examples from the way they bring up their children to manage multinationals. Admittedly, such examples do not reflect the run-of-the-mill management book, but they are too significant to ignore. Take, for example, this remark, which comes from a senior manager of a large international retail company with whom we have worked closely for many years.

> We're all big boys in the board of management and don't easily share things – but this works well. The closer you get to the top, the easier the world becomes as far as values are concerned. It is as if you are back with your family. Honesty, clarity, trust, consistency, being strict and fair, sticking to agreements, self-knowledge, humor, acceptance, success, and failure…these sorts of things may be given an elegant wrapping by management, but essentially it all comes down to being a good parent.

In this book, you will find no tricks, tips, or quick fixes for running an organization; instead, I have tried to make the underlying principles as clear as possible. I will try to show why people feel safe or not, and why they are motivated, creative, depressive, loyal, and open to change or not.

This is an optimistic book. During my investigation into the roots of the human capacity for attachment and exploration, I have become convinced that integrity and ethical – in other words, decent – leadership ultimately provide the center of rest that people in organizations need if they are to continue functioning and exploring in times of increasing turbulence.

In Chapter 1, we discuss the S-curve and the treacherous rigidity it can cause. In Chapter 2, we discuss the nature and the functioning of the attachment and exploration systems, both of which show how we can escape from the rigidity that arises within the S-curve. Chapter 3 deals with consistency as the most natural way of influencing attachment and exploration. Chapter 4 makes a detour and deals with attachment to people and attachment to matter. This acts as an introduction to Chapter 5, in which we discuss growth in maturity, within the framework of dealing with complexity. Chapter 6 focuses on diversity and makes it a concrete success factor for change. Chapter 7 shows the importance of internal communication for maintaining external consistency.

I look back with considerable pleasure and gratitude on all the help that I have received from so many people. First of all, to Ann and Richard, who have always forgiven my "unforgivable" sin of simultaneously starting a book, the research for a management tool (the AEM-Cube®), and a consultancy business. I am particularly grateful to those who finally made this publication possible: Hans Ritman, Raymond Gijsen, and Jonathan Ellis. Hans has always had the patience to press ahead despite the sin I have just mentioned. The book should have been finished a lot sooner. Many have given me valuable feedback. I cannot mention everybody, but I should like to name a few: Gert Jan de Kruyff, Ernst Horwitz, Bob Sadler, Niek Sniekers, Fiona Henderson, David Lewis, Rick Price, Annika Ratcliffe, Maarten Kouwenhoven, Mitch Kotula, Sheila Cox, Jantien Fennema, Mirjam Ietswaart, Michel Evers, Philip Idenburg, Peter van den Akker, Mike Jeans, Peter Woltman, Jim Arena, Barbara Braun, David Thomson, and Drew Watson.

1. *Success Is a Sleeping Pill*

THIS chapter deals first with change as a prerequisite for survival. I then discuss the "rhythm" of growth and decline in everything – from nature through the life of people to the life of organizations – as sketched by the well-known *S-curve*. Using the idea of the S-curve, in combination with the ideas of *feedforward* and *feedback*, we can understand how the future always allows itself to be overtaken, as it were, by the past. But also, how managers can arm themselves with the *feedforward hierarchy* against the "assassin" known as the past, and use it to give their organizations the ability to start new innovations ahead of time...and thus escape from the "prison" of the S-curve, to escape, indeed, from *S-catraz*.

CHANGE AS A PREREQUISITE FOR SURVIVAL

"Continuous change," "the need for a company to be constantly alert to profit from movements in the market" – we've heard these phrases so many times that they have become clichés. Yet if we take a good look around us, we will acknowledge how difficult it is to put these clichés into practice. We all have examples of companies getting stuck – where rules, procedures, and internal power politics have become more important in day-to-day operations than looking for new ways of serving customers and keeping costs to a minimum.

The following example shows that even an organization such as Hewlett-Packard (HP) can find itself trapped in a mental "Alcatraz." We will regularly refer to Hewlett-Packard in this chapter, because it not only has examples of rigidity in its history, but also is an example of how a company can constantly regenerate itself. In their best seller *Built to Last*, James Collins and Jerry Porras describe the results of their research into companies that have the ability continually to reinvent themselves. Hewlett-Packard, they conclude, belongs to the "best of the best."[1] When Carly Fiorina took over the helm from Lew Platt in the summer of 1999, the authoritative American business magazine *Business Week* was less than enthusiastic.[2] Hewlett-Packard, according to *Business Week*, had developed into an organization of 130 different product groups with a "suffocating" bureaucracy. A former member of the board illustrated the company's increasing bureaucracy with an anecdote about four managers of the retail chain Best Buy Co. They wanted to purchase a few computer products from Hewlett-Packard and were bombarded by no less than 50 (!) employees, each praising the products of their various divisions. The culture of consensus that had developed over the years within Hewlett-Packard had also undermined the innovation potential of the company, according to *Business Week*, which stated: "HP hasn't had a mega-breakthrough product since the inkjet printer was introduced in 1984." The managers did not dare to invest in new ideas, because they were scared that they would then not reach their targets for the next quarter, according to the magazine.

A particularly good example of this is provided by a former research employee at Hewlett-Packard, Ira P. Goldstein. In the early 1990s Goldstein developed a prototype for a Web browser, and in 1993 he showed it to the then top man, Platt. Platt was enthusiastic and told Goldstein to show his development to the computer division. After that, the idea died a silent death. "They didn't see how it could help them sell more computers," wrote Goldstein some time later. Two years later, Netscape became the first Internet superstar with its Navigator browser.

A tale such as this about Goldstein and his browser that died a silent death speaks volumes about the situation of the company and its management. The enthusiasm that Platt showed for Goldstein's invention was quite simply no match for the rigidity that had taken hold of the organization. Perhaps Platt was fully aware of where Hewlett-Packard stood and where he would like to take the company. But it seems that he, in common with much of the organization, had become trapped in the quagmire into which the company had fallen. Platt, who had been with the company for 33 years, had no idea how to handle the situation, according to *Business Week*. Despite the lack of new products, the magazine suggested, he was still unable to develop a policy that would entice people to leave their cubbyholes. The then new top woman, Fiorina, had a heavy task ahead of her, wrote the magazine; she would have to revitalize the heavy culture of HP in the first few months and show them how to develop the sort of speed that was required in the Internet era.

The departing CEO had become part of the system. A new CEO was needed – one who could act as a breath of fresh air within the organization. But what could have been done to prevent Fiorina becoming, in the course of time, part of the Hewlett-Packard system? She is, after all, only human.

Aren't people always inclined to relax their mental defenses when things are going well, as if enjoying a summer's day? Aren't people inclined to stick to a "success formula" and therefore lapse into rigidity? What causes this process of relaxing mental defenses and lapsing into rigidity? And if we can find an answer to this, can we free ourselves from them, or are we in a mental Alcatraz from which escape is impossible? We will first take a look at this last question. Then we will look at what effects those beautiful summer days of success have on a company's ability to change.

There is, indeed, a mental Alcatraz where we all, regardless of who we are, keep finding ourselves trapped. It is almost as if the wages of success are paid in the currency of rigidity. It is as if, in our struggle for success, we are constantly ambushed by an invisible enemy, who lulls us to sleep before we are aware of it. When we wake up, the world has changed and our success has evaporated.

THE S-CURVE: THE RHYTHM OF GROWTH AND DECLINE

A practical way of applying the well-known concept of renewal, growth, and decay to management practices is the *S-curve*. The S-curve plots the process of decline and resurrection; it is the rhythm of the seasons that can be identified in everything that grows. This book is about people and organizations, but they do not have a monopoly on the S-curve. Whether we talk about the rise and fall of societies or Mafia godfathers; rabbit colonies; love relationships; the life cycle of DeskJet printers; our own career; or the course of epidemics: S-curves reveal the dynamics (Figure 1.1 – the vertical axis indicates the growth, the horizontal axis the time from left to right).

The S-curve has appeared increasingly in management books over the last few years. Theodore Modis describes the S-curve for companies in his book *Conquering Uncertainty*. He uses the cycle of seasons: winter, spring, summer, fall, winter, spring, and so on.

> *Winter.* In the winter, companies have time to develop new ideas, but profitability is poor. There is chaos and uncertainty. Death lies in wait. This gives a sense of urgency to keep on looking for solutions and finally to make choices.
> *Spring.* The advantage of spring is enthusiasm. The disadvantage is that it demands high levels of investment. Innovative concepts are turned into tangible products and services. It is the period of "upscaling."

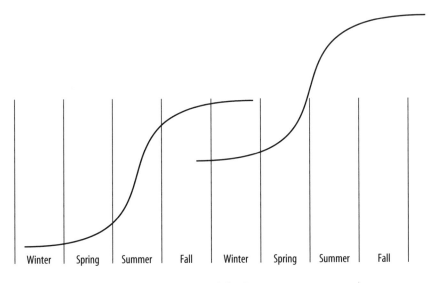

Figure 1.1 *The S-curve*

Summer. This is the time of production. Logistics, technique, and commerce all support the chosen direction. Investments are less important; profitability assumes center stage. The innovative people who were around at the start have disappeared; controllers and bureaucrats have taken their place. This is the stage that sees the increase in rules and procedures aimed at increasing efficiency.

Fall. In this stage, the first signs of decline become apparent. The company may, for example, start losing market share. Initially, decline is repudiated and reasons are given from all sides to explain why things are going wrong. But eventually, fear and anxiety can no longer be ignored and this can even give rise to panic. The solutions are downsizing, tightening the belt, pressing the last bit of profit from products, "back to basics," and so on.[3]

Nobel Prize winners such as Jacques Monod and Ilya Prigogine have shown in their work how, in light of the relationships described in the S-curve, order can emerge from chaos.[4] This concept has been translated for management by an increasing number of writers, particularly in the 1990s. Authors such as Kenneth Blanchard, Terry Waghorn, Charles Handy, and Theodore Modis have demonstrated how the S-curve is and should be part of the armory of every leader, manager, and strategist.[5] Marc van der Erve has described how values and norms shift within the S-curve.[6] Jeffrey P. Shay and Frank T. Rothaermel sketch in an article how the S-curve provides a basic structure that allows existing models for strategy-forming (including the growth and market-share matrix of the Boston Consulting

Group) to be linked together, resulting in a broader and far more dynamic model for strategic analysis.[7]

For writer Theodore Modis, originally a physicist, it is an excellent measuring tool that allows the formulation of exceptionally reliable prognoses: "This curve can be used quantitatively to achieve predictability and deep insights. DEC saved many millions in 1985 by accurately predicting how much turnover could be generated from servicing an old product...In 1992, the British government, to give another example, could have spared itself the pain of attempting to close down two-thirds of the coal mines."[8] Theodore Modis also applies similar mathematical calculations to the careers of individuals, such as Hemingway, Hitchcock, and Mozart. Using the S-curve for the works of Mozart, Modis calculates that the first 18 compositions were probably never written down due to "technical" problems: The young Mozart could not write well enough, nor speak well enough to dictate them to his father. Most authors, however, do *not* approach the S-curve in such a strict mathematical way, but make use of a "qualitative and subjective approach." In this book, we, too, use a conceptual approach to the S-curve rather than the strict mathematical approach adopted by Modis.

S-CURVES AND PEOPLE

The S-curve also applies to the lives of people. Take the S-curve of a relationship (perhaps a caricature, but certainly nothing out of the ordinary): We fall in love, maybe emerging from a winter of solitude, and find ourselves in the spring of happiness. We dream about a future that ends "They lived happily ever after." We develop from being a couple in love, move in together, and become partners for life. And all the time we are getting to know each other better and better. We learn about irritations and weaknesses, and about the areas where interests conflict and where polarization is possible. Initially these are dismissed; they do not fit into our perception. After a while, the novelty wears off and the many advantages are taken for granted. Perhaps the next move is a marriage, children, a mortgage, two careers – and our days are filled with things that we had never imagined.

Is this all there is? Is this the way it was supposed to be? A pattern of disagreement, stress, dissatisfaction, and frustration shakes us awake, and for the first time we look around at a world we had never discussed, never dreamed about – and yet apparently we had worked towards it. We were happy with our marriage, happy with our children, happy with our mortgage, happy with our careers. But everything that used to please us now appears to have a reverse side, and all those reverses together feel like a straitjacket. *He* was pleased with her ambition, but now she refuses to give up her job, and that causes a dilemma: Do you take that international promotion or not? *She* was pleased with his ideas about emancipation, but when push comes to shove, he refuses to accept responsibility. The relationship has moved through an S-curve. How it continues remains to be seen: Either it comes to an end, or a new S-curve begins.

During our lives, we pass through dozens of such S-curves. The S-curve of our infancy, elementary school, high school, relationships with friends, study, first job, second job, third job, marriage…

S-CURVES IN ORGANIZATIONS

There are enough recent examples of companies having become too rigid to react to important technological change that they found themselves playing catch-up in a race they could probably never win. Merrill Lynch resisted share-trading over the Internet for four years. And all the while, new and existing companies, such as E-Trade, Charles Schwab, and smaller discount brokers had captured market share with an efficient and cheap formula for buying and selling shares. Merrill Lynch was so hostile to the Internet that vice president and head of share-trading John "Launny" Steffens publicly announced in August 1998 that share-trading over the Internet "should be seen as a serious threat to the financial position of the American citizen." The paralysis at Merrill Lynch was not, however, caused by any concern for the public good, but was a result of the internal corporate culture. The contingent of 15,000 powerful traders was petrified that share-trading over the Internet would erode its income from commissions, which made up 30% of its total earnings; it resisted such a development by tooth and nail.

Merrill Lynch is by no means the only reputable company that has been held back by its own culture. When Amazon.com opened its Internet trading in 1995, Barnes & Noble refused to take this new form of "e-tailing" seriously. This leading chain of bookstores had just experienced a period of fevered growth. Barnes & Noble had, for example, just started innovative cafés and music shops in its large stores. Internally, so much attention was directed at expanding the physical chains that people were totally blind to the possibility of an alternate supply chain. It took two years for Barnes & Noble hesitantly to open the doors of its own virtual store – Barnesandnoble.com. This delay has proved damaging to Barnes & Noble.[9]

"Seasons" are not the biggest challenge facing us, either in companies or in our lives. It isn't about how we can protect the existing against decline – decline can't be stopped – but, rather, about how we handle the rhythm of the seasons.

If we just allow the rise and fall to take its own course, then the curve will go downwards at approximately the same rate that it went upwards. The total curve will follow the bell-shaped movement of the classic product life cycle (Figure 1.2).

Now we return to our previous question: Why is it so difficult to remain flexible, to escape from the mental Alcatraz? The answer is found in the idea that many people have that summer will never end and in their inclination to keep a firm grasp on success. People construct their own mental Alcatraz. As the line of the S-curve rises, when success comes to complete fruition, then you step into Alcatraz – or more appropriately in this context – *S-catraz*. At the end of the rising S-curve, success smiles on you, and nothing indicates the possibility of decline. The fact that the high of success makes itself felt is actually the first signal that decline is imminent. Bernardo Bertolucci describes this poetically thus: "decline of which you are not aware, the decline of those that look but do not see, who listen but do not hear, of those who do not know how to judge themselves or others."[10]

Richard D'Aveni, author of the management best seller *Hypercompetition: Managing the Dynamics of Strategic Maneuvering*, recounted during a lecture in 1996 that Peter Drucker had, after reading his book, invited him to dinner. On that occasion, Drucker is said to have remarked, "If the gods wish to destroy you, they give you twenty years of

There seem to be only two directions: up or down

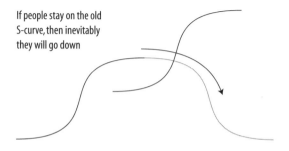

If people stay on the old
S-curve, then inevitably
they will go down

Figure 1.2 *The path of the S-curve*

success."[11] In other words, the summer of success can lull people to sleep. And success is what it is all about in the second or upper part of the S-curve. All efforts in the first half of the curve (the bottom part) are directed at harvesting in the second half (the upper part). Even at the very moment that the growth curve – which describes the life cycle of a product, an organization, or anything else – is about to flatten out, everything still seems to be in order. Success still seems assured.

Gary Hamel, C. K. Prahalad, and many others suggest, in relationship to strategic renewal, that success is one of the major threats to true organizational change.[12] Their vision can easily be coupled to the S-curve. Hamel and Prahalad concentrate on two aspects. First, that people experiencing success have little appetite for distancing themselves from a successful past, and second, that people continue to concentrate on repeating and continuing success into the future. This makes them more focused on (the success of) yesterday than on the demands of tomorrow.

In itself, the observation that success lulls people to sleep is a letdown. The problem is well known. This rational knowledge seems insufficient to prevent rigidity, the sleep at the end of the S-curve. This is due to the devious way in which the process works. Nobody is aware of the exact moment they fall asleep. It's the same with an organization: When renewal is required, there is the danger that it will simply fall asleep without noticing. Similarly, a company can suddenly wake up disoriented and rub its eyes as it takes in the unknown surroundings in which it finds itself.

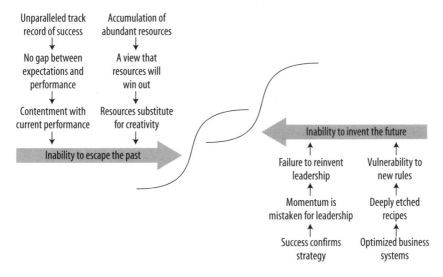

Figure 1.3 *Wish me 20 years of success (Gary Hamel and C. K. Prahalad)*

In other words, S-catraz is difficult to avoid because the road leading to it is paved with success and because that success, slowly but surely, will turn against the organization. The situation described here (schematically shown in Figure 1.3) is cleverly captured in the work of the Dutch graphic artist M. C. Escher; one of his works shows the subtle and imperceptible transformation of white horses into black ones (Figure 1.4).

In this work by Escher, a group of white knights on white horses rides across the page from left to right and about halfway up seems to evaporate into black knights on black horses riding in the opposite direction. This image of a "white" force changing almost imperceptibly into a "black" force perfectly symbolizes how initial proponents of change – at the bottom of the S-curve when an organization is still in its infancy – imperceptibly change into a force that opposes change.

The image by Escher is all the more appropriate because the moment of change is so intangible. The same happens in organizations. Initially (at the start of the S-curve), factors such as structure and procedure are the allies of growth for the emerging organization. At the start of the S-curve, the "spring," there is a need for enthusiasm and optimism but, at the same time, a considerable need for the right investments in structures. It seems as if everything has to happen at once, each aspect intertwined with the other: marketing, production, sales, service, aftersales, planning, logistics,

Figure 1.4 *Escher's trap* (M. C. Escher, *Regular Division of the Plane III*)

distribution, legal affairs, and staff matters. Any solution that helps structure this chaos and increase efficiency is welcomed with open arms. Structure is the friend of everything in the stage of development: It provides strength, effectiveness, efficiency, security, quality, and predictability.

Somewhere in this process, however, structure becomes a burden; entrepreneurs and specialists turn into controllers and bureaucrats. Somewhere in this process, and nobody can say with certainty at what time or on what day it happens, the white horses suddenly turn black. There are still a lot of resources available, functions are easily thought up, and one rule more or less won't make all that much difference – even though it may slow down the decision-making process. Everything, it seems, is possible, and then all at once it becomes too much, everything boils over, and it takes ages to reach decisions.

In other words, suddenly and without warning, those initial advocates of change turn into forces that oppose change with every means at their disposal. This also happens within the people in the organization itself: The process is largely a mental one and is reflected in the way people think about and look at the world around them. People become lazy; the structures that have arisen around them make things all too easy for them. What's more, success feeds vanity. The reward of success has become a sleeping pill, the befuddled senses that follow a bottle of good wine. The hangover comes the next day, when you wake up and find yourself in a strange room.

To summarize: During the course of the S-curve, those factors that were critical and essential for initial success become an impediment to change. What is so treacherous about all this is that it takes place as slowly and as imperceptibly as the transformation of Escher's horses. Friends who took care of structures and procedures, and thus helped words to become deeds, change into enemies of change because they consider those structures and procedures as ends in themselves.

FEEDFORWARD AND FEEDBACK, OR HOW THE FUTURE ALLOWS ITSELF TO BE OVERTAKEN BY THE PAST

Life is a moment in space, when the dream has gone, it's a lonelier place...
Barbra Streisand[13]

The course of the S-curve in organizations can become more tangible – and thus better manageable – if we look at it with two ideas in the back of our minds: *feedforward* and *feedback*. Feedforward and feedback are not only important concepts for understanding the gradual rigidity that takes hold of an organization in the process sketched above. We shall also refer to these ideas in the coming chapters when we discuss the way in which people have handled change and the fear of the unknown for millions of years. *Feedforward* and *feedback* are terms derived from systems theory.

FEEDBACK: TAKE A SHOWER IN AN OLD HOTEL

Everybody knows feedback systems. The systems for controlling the refrigerator and the central heating are both good examples. The human body is full of feedback systems, which control such things as blood pressure, the heart rate, and blood sugar levels. The following illustration – one that has been used on many occasions – shows clearly how a feedback system works.

You are a guest in an ancient British castle that has been redeveloped as a hotel. The cavernous bathroom has a large bath in it, and above that bath are two taps. Somewhere deep down in the bowels of the hotel is a boiler or gas water heater that provides the building with hot water. You turn on the taps, and the shower starts pouring down cold water – exactly what you would expect. You wait for some time and then decide to turn up the hot tap and/or turn down the cold tap. Suddenly, the water is scalding hot, and you quickly turn down the hot tap. Then the water turns ice-cold. You turn up the hot tap. If your stay is short, then you'll probably never get the hang of the system. If you're fortunate enough to spend some time there, then you'll probably get to know how long it takes for the system to react to a turn of the tap.

This example shows how preoccupied you are with the past. The temperature of the water in the shower is not the same as the temperature of the water that leaves the boiler at that moment. If you don't know how much delay there is in the system, then you can't really control the process. An additional factor is that the greater the delay in the system, the more difficult it is to control that system.

The essence of feedback is that the action is directed at achieving (again) a situation that existed in the past or that meets a standard set in the past (in this case, a comfortable shower temperature of 38°C). *Feedback* means "control using information from the past." There are two forms of feedback: *reinforcing feedback* and *balancing feedback*. *Reinforcing feedback* is "feedback that strengthens itself." A product is a hit, people starting talking about it to each other, more people buy it, more people talk to each other about it, and so on (think of the sayings "success breeds success" or "money makes money"). *Balancing feedback* is "feedback that produces stability." The temperature in a room is maintained at a constant level, the car stays inside the white lines, a project remains within budget.

During the first stage of the S-curve, reinforcing feedback is predominant, ensuring that success breeds more success; in the second stage of the S-curve, balancing feedback takes over. For example, competitors may have entered the market, and everybody in the market is keeping their eyes on everybody else. If one tinkers with the price, the rest follow suit.

FEEDFORWARD: FROM AMSTERDAM TO PARIS

Feedforward is another form of control, which arises out of our ability to anticipate the future. It is as if the future is pulled back in order to control the present. *Feedback* is all about control based on information from the past; *feedforward* is control based on the expectations, hopes, dreams, and wishes people want to achieve in the future. An example will make this clear. Let's imagine a driver – and, admittedly, this is an extreme example – who constantly drives his car around a traffic circle (Figure 1.5, left). This driver bases his actions purely on feedback. He pays attention to the lines on the road and makes use of the accelerator using feedback information (from the speedometer on the dashboard and the position of the car on the road) about the existing requirements (the maximum speed and the white lines on the road).

In a feedforward situation (Figure 1.5, right), the driver is not going around a traffic circle, but has decided to drive from Amsterdam to Paris. Feedforward bases control on information it receives from the future. In a feedback situation, actions are directed at *reestablishing* a situation that

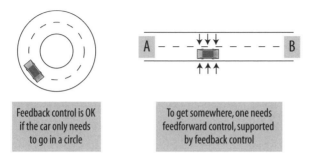

Figure 1.5 *Feedforward and feedback control*

had occurred in the past; in a feedforward situation, actions are directed at *reaching* a goal that does not yet exist, a vision of the future. But not everything directed at a future aim is governed by feedforward. The aim of achieving an annual growth in turnover of, say, 10% is, without any further information about the higher aim and deeper intention of such growth, and without any additional information about the *context* of this aim, the same as the white line on the road: a rule that has to be followed.

The power of the feedforward direction expresses itself in self-fulfilling prophecies: If we start our day thinking that things will go well, they generally will; if, however, we start the day thinking that things will go badly, then again, they generally will. Pribram[14] has pointed out the fundamental difference between feedback and feedforward. He says that feedback has little to do with *information*: The driver who goes around the traffic circle only needs information about his position on the road in relation to the white lines. He could even drive blindfold, with a passenger who gives instructions such as "a little to the left" and "a little to the right." Some managers think that when they are controlling budgets they are dealing with information. This is not true. All they are doing is judging figures against a norm that has already been set. The essential difference is that feedback-oriented work is directed by a signal (a deviation in the budget), while feedforward-oriented work is directed at the content, about the *why* of the budget and about the context in which that budget is placed.

Feedforward is based on our ability to imagine the future and to anticipate it. This can have negative results – think, for example, about the fear of failure: We see failure looming up in front of us, and that makes things go

Accents at the beginning and end of the S-curve

Start of S-curve: Feedforward impulses	End of S-curve: Feedback impulses
Impulses are based on the future, on something that is not yet present	Impulses are based on the past, through feedback with something that has taken place
Cause little or no delay in either time or space	Cause delay since the feedback always takes time
Deal with something that is still to come but doesn't yet exist	Deal with concrete and tangible matters
Start and finish	Can continue endlessly
Change a condition	Maintain an existing condition
Are dependent on information that gives a "direction" or "goal"; without specific contextual information about the direction, there can be no feedforward	Are dependent on a signal that indicates a "difference" or "deviation"; as long as that takes place, no further information about the type or nature of the information is essential

Table 1.1 *The differences between feedback and feedforward*

wrong. The positive side is that a strong vision, dream, or idea about the future can drive us forward. It can lead us down the road towards the realization of our dream.

Table 1.1 shows the differences between feedback and feedforward.

THE FEEDFORWARD HIERARCHY: A PRACTICAL APPROACH TO MANAGING THE S-CURVE

The concept of the S-curve can be made more tangible – and more importantly, more applicable – if we use terms that are part of our day-to-day vocabulary: *strategy, norms, vision, dreams, process, structure, ideas, tactics, actions, procedures, mission*. When I ask managers to list these terms in order from *feedforward* to *feedback*, they generally produce a list much like the one shown in Figure 1.6.

This feedforward hierarchy describes the S-curve, from the bottom upwards. The feedforward hierarchy gives managers a lever they can use to move their company, department, or project further up the S-curve, and thus promote development. When a project is in the early stages of development, the manager has to apply downward pressure on the lever: from values to dream to vision and so on. The more feedback the manager receives, the more tangible the project becomes for the organization. Once the project has become concrete, top management will increasingly delegate the leadership of the project to middle-management levels lower down in the organization. In other words, the organization will move step by step from feedforward to

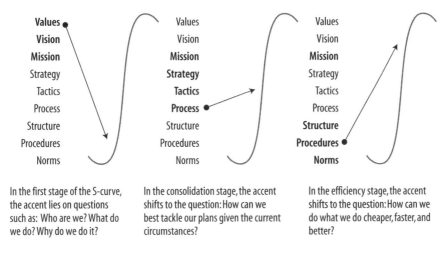

In the first stage of the S-curve, the accent lies on questions such as: Who are we? What do we do? Why do we do it?

In the consolidation stage, the accent shifts to the question: How can we best tackle our plans given the current circumstances?

In the efficiency stage, the accent shifts to the question: How can we do what we do cheaper, faster, and better?

Figure 1.6 *The feedforward hierarchy as a way of mapping the S-curve*

feedback. This happens as gradually as in Escher's print, where the white knights and horses gradually transform themselves into black knights and horses. This process is also essential: The more concrete a project becomes, the greater the feedback. Those "black horses" are not only inevitable, they are also useful. Success is "bought" with an increase in rigidity. Profitable operations are simply not possible without rules and feedback. Management's task is to accept this while remaining above it and anticipating it.

Values and norms

Any discussion with management about the order of the individual terms generally turns into a heated debate about the proper position of the term *values*. This is hardly surprising, since generally (and certainly in the Netherlands) *values* and *norms* are lumped together – almost as if they were synonyms. Yet when I demonstrate things with real examples, we generally reach the conclusion that *values* should be at the top of the list. For example, respect or honesty says something about the way you should act – and for this reason they seem to set a norm (in short, the highest form of feedback). But values have a "thou shalt" character, while norms have a "thou shalt not" character. Values give direction (information about the future, even if this is rather abstract), but say little about the way in which the direction is achieved. Norms provide a boundary, and are generally concrete in the way they mark this boundary. Norms are always derived from values: "Don't lie" (a norm) is derived from "integrity" and "showing respect for each other" (values). On the other hand, somebody with values such as "integrity" and "showing respect for each other" may well occasionally lie – there are situations in which this is appropriate. The classic example is hiding Jews during World War II: In such a situation there is justification, taking into account values, for breaking the norm about not telling lies. Anybody who rigidly sticks to the norm and by doing so betrays the Jews would no longer be considered a person of "integrity" or somebody who shows respect for others.

This sort of discussion usually results in managers reaching the conclusion that *values* should top the list in the feedforward hierarchy. Norms, on the other hand, can be compared with traffic signs, or with the white lines on the road. They show what can and cannot be done. Values, to continue the traffic metaphor, are the *reason* you are on the road, the destination you wish to reach.

At the top, the feedforward hierarchy is concerned with the future and is abstract (values, vision). At the bottom, it is concerned with the past; it is concrete by nature and control-driven (procedures, norms). A fine practical example of the feedforward hierarchy is to be found in a speech given by Carly Fiorina, former CEO of Hewlett-Packard, to the annual general meeting of shareholders held on February 29, 2000, at Cupertino (California). In this speech, Fiorina wanders from the distant future (an advance on the next S-curve) to the present (results of the quarter that had just been concluded). The subheadings show which part of the feedforward hierarchy is being discussed.

Values

"HP is indeed a great company. It is a company that I have admired from afar, if you will, for many years. It is a company that I have admired for its values. The values of trust, integrity, teamwork, contribution. And it is a company that I admire greatly for its inventive capability…As we reinvent ourselves we are, in fact, in many real ways, drawing from our history and our traditions to help us in that reinvention. I believe that Hewlett-Packard has a unique opportunity to become what I would call, what many of us at HP now call, an e-company with a shining soul…We are blessed with a company that was given a very strong soul and spirit and character by Bill Hewlett and Dave Packard. And it is the nature of that soul that helps us now in our reinvention…

"So I'd like first to start by sharing with you the rules of the garage, as we call them at HP now…Our phrase for that inside HP today is 'Preserve the best and reinvent the rest.' And if you look at these rules I think you will see that all of them come from the great legacy that Bill and Dave left us. We talk here first about an environment in which every employee believes that their contribution can make a real difference. And so our first rule, as you see here, is believe you can change the world…

"And coupled with that, believe you can change the world, is another rule at the end which says that believe together we can do anything. Because of course, teamwork is at the heart of all great reinvention…You will also see that we think speed is essential…Trust is important, as we talk about keeping the tools unlocked…Trust in sharing with our colleagues. And of course, a customer defines a job well done. And throughout it all we remember, for ourselves, for our customers, and for our share owners, that this is a company founded by inventors. And that it is fundamentally our inventive capacity which distinguishes us from our competitors. Which continues to allow us to make a contribution to our share owners and to our customers."

Vision

"As we move forward in this reinvention phase, we are constantly aware of the fact that we are now competing in a very different era. We believe, and others in our industry believe, that in fact the pure product era has come to a close. Every product now is more valuable based upon the types of services that are wrapped around that product. Whether we're talking about a printer that has with it a service of personalized news…In fact, what is happening today is products are more and more valuable to the extent that they are networked and to the extent that they are included in a package of services. And so it's vital for us, as a company, to not only continue in our strong tradition of product generation, but also to put those products together with services. E-services is, we believe, the next great movement in the networked economy… So the challenge for us in HP is to play uniquely in driving this e-services world."

Mission

"We believe HP is uniquely positioned at the intersection of these services, these assets or processes that can be turned into services, to deliver over a network. The infrastructure that supports those services, and the appliances, the information appliances. Whether those are PCs or cell phones or wrist watches, or a microchip so tiny that it can be embedded in literally every device. It is our privilege and our competitive advantage to play at the intersection of those services. The infrastructure that supports it and the information appliances that deliver those services. So it is our job to use that privileged position to drive revenue opportunities and profit opportunities as we help transform our customers' businesses."

Strategy

"So we are really focused on six strategic priorities today. First, I would say that we are focused on increasing the performance from our current core businesses…Second strategic priority is to eliminate a lot of replication and redundancy and inefficiency that has grown up in our business…Third, we must refocus our energies on providing a total customer experience that competitively advantages us…Fourth, we have a very efficient business in many ways, in terms of inventory management as an example…And priorities five and six really come back to the notions I was talking about earlier…

"So these are the strategic priorities that we are focused on as a business. These are the priorities that allow us to both reinvent the company and produce superior competitive results in the year 2000 and beyond."

Tactics

"One of the things that we've done is fairly fundamentally realign our business. And we've realigned our business so that we are both world-class providers of technology and products and solutions, and world-class providers of a total customer experience. We have created two product and technology generation engines…

"In addition, we have formed two organizations that are focused on providing the best total customer experience."

Operational matters (process, structure, procedures)

"So these are the…fundamental building blocks now within HP. World class product generation, world class customer experience. And of course, HP Labs is at the center of all of this. HP Labs is the place where our inventive capability begins and is perhaps best personified. And we're focused very much now on taking the technology and the capability of HP Labs and moving it more quickly into the businesses and out into the marketplace. I mentioned our deal with Kodak and I want to focus on this just for a moment…Another important deal that we announced relatively recently was with Ford Motor Company."

Norms

"And finally to update you on how we have performed over this first quarter in 2000, I will say that we have committed to our share owners for 2000 that we will provide revenue and profit growth in the 12–15% range…We believe we've made good progress in our first quarter against that goal. As you can see, overall revenues were up 14%…From an operating income perspective, we are two cents above analysts' expectations at 80 cents. Our reported earnings were 77 cents…And I might just add that our stock closed today at $134.8." [Applause]

THE PROFESSION OF LEADER FROM THE PERSPECTIVE OF THE S-CURVE

I have sat and watched the chairman of a great company speak to his assembled barons. "I have two messages for you today," he said. "First, I want to remind you that we are a very successful business, perhaps more successful today than we have ever been. Second, I must tell you that if we want to continue to be successful we shall have to change, fundamentally, the way we are working now."

Charles Handy[15]

In practice, management is all about juggling measures directed at either feedforward or feedback. Results-oriented managers and leaders will always feel a certain pressure to make things concrete and tangible. Feedforward indicates the reason for action and the direction it takes; feedback is essential for keeping everything on track and making sure that the goals set are actually reached. Concentrating solely on feedforward is something for dreamers, isolated from the real world; pure feedback is the reserve of bureaucrats.

At the start of the S-curve, very little is tangible. In the fragile early stages of the growth curve, people who can "see" what isn't there yet (literally, people with vision) are worth their weight in gold. The future has to be brought back to the present. Once the ideas have been given some sort of reality, the visionaries have done their job, and operators take over the responsibilities of production. Visionaries think in terms of *feedforward*, that is, about things that are yet to happen. Operators think in terms of *feedback*, that is, about controlling and checking that everything works as it should.

Actual management takes place on a sliding scale that shifts from feedforward to feedback, from fantasy to reality. The paradox is that with each new piece of reality and each new success in achieving that ideal vision, people accept a slight increase in feedback – people want to maintain the success, to "freeze" it in rules – and so allow events to be increasingly directed by the past. You can't escape it. In reality, success is bought in control terms with a little feedback, a little rigidity. Every further step along the scale, that sliding scale from feedforward to feedback, demands sacrificing a little bit of future-oriented behavior, increases slightly the rigidity, and makes people more self-satisfied because they have reached a milestone.

Perhaps this is superfluous: For an individual product, this process is unavoidable. There comes a moment when the product is (more or less) fully developed, and the "engine" is humming along nicely in the market. For that specific product the following holds true: Make the production as efficient as possible, increase profitability, and (finally) decide when the curtain has to fall as the product life cycle draws to an end. For an organization as a whole, this does not mean the final curtain must fall, as long as it makes sure there are other products and services in various stages of development. (This idea is as old as the famous matrix of the Boston Consulting Group.) If management does not pay attention to this, then the *entire* organization will move too far up the curve and could find itself in a life-threatening situation.

It is advisable to take steps to ensure that a new S-curve has started before the existing one has reached the top of its profitability. There are means (in an organization) and spirit (in a marriage) to support such a new development. Each S-curve passes the baton on to the next one

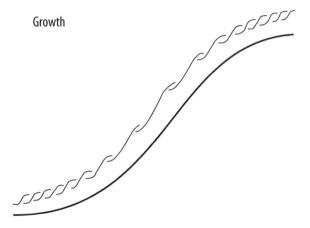

Growth

Figure 1.7 *Growth* (Theodore Modis, *Conquering Uncertainty*)

(Figure 1.7).

A proactive agenda for change and growth has the following four priorities.

1 Create an image of a new future direction.
2 Profit for as long and as much as possible from the advantages of the old S-curve.
3 Demolish what should be removed and retain what is valuable.
4 Manage the transformation.

These points are shown in Figure 1.8. The "harvest–invest" axis, which runs down the right-hand side of Figure 1.8, shows that investments must be made at the beginning of an S-curve. At the start of the sharply perpendicular line – if things go well – the first encouraging reports will filter in; during periods of transformation, profit is seldom made. At the end of the S-curve, profits will begin to decline.

If management does not pay constant attention to this agenda of construction, transformation, and destruction of different S-curves in the organization, if management does not – before the decay process sets in – start building up the next S-curve, then the existing projects, products, organizational units, and so on will die, but no new S-curves will enter the pipeline. If products and programs are not destroyed at the end of their lifetime, then they will generally remain: They do not contribute very much, but they do keep employees at work, demand attention from management, and cost money. And the result is a situation in which all the products of a company are at the top of the S-curve simultaneously. This

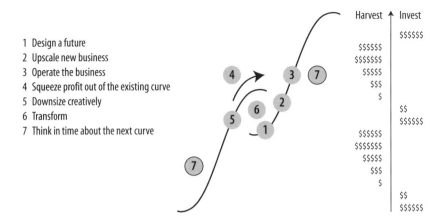

1 Design a future
2 Upscale new business
3 Operate the business
4 Squeeze profit out of the existing curve
5 Downsize creatively
6 Transform
7 Think in time about the next curve

Figure 1.8 *The agenda of the leader*

brings the whole organization into mortal danger.

This book, however, is not about portfolio management. This book is about the elements that determine an organization's ability to spring from one (nearly) completed S-curve to the start of another S-curve, and thus escape from S-catraz, the prison of mental rigidity that seems inevitably connected with success.

The management of this escape from S-catraz, this struggle against Escher's black knights, is a top priority for leaders of any organization. If they are to escape from S-catraz, managers and employees need to let go of the old, with all the fear that this entails, and at the same time set off towards a new future, in which fear and hope of a new success both play a role. Giving people the power to finish their own S-curve, let go, and start again is a core competency in the struggle against the black knights of organizational rigidity. The following speech by Carly Fiorina serves as a good example.

> It is a great pleasure to be with you today, our valued partners and our inventive colleagues. What I'd like to do today is talk with you about the spirit of invention. A spirit that I believe is necessary for all of us to thrive and prosper in this new net economy. A spirit that is necessary to help us adjust to all the changes in the net economy. And I think it's fitting in a way that we should take our inspiration this morning from the place in which we sit, the Louvre, arguably the most extraordinary collection, the extraordinary celebration of human ingenuity and creativity and inventiveness in the world. And as we reflect on this market as we reflect on the dynamics of the net economy, the promise of e-services, we can learn from one of the greatest inventors ever,
>
> Leonardo da Vinci.

Now as we sit here in the Louvre, you might think of Leonardo da Vinci as the painter of the *Mona Lisa* and, of course, he was that, but he was also much more. He was perhaps one of the greatest inventors of our time. Though while he spent 50%, approximately, of his time painting, he spent the rest of his time inventing. Inventing new products, inventing new prophecies, inventing new theories.

Now in his famous notebooks, da Vinci tells a story of approaching a cave. And as he approaches this dark cave he is overcome by true emotions. One emotion of fear, the fear of what might be inside this dark and mysterious and somewhat threatening cave. And the other emotion desire, desire to see whether there is something miraculous and wonderful in this dark and mysterious cave. And I think these two twin emotions of fear and desire have much to teach us about how we as companies must adapt to the new net economy, to the new Millennium, to all of the challenges, the promises and yes the threats of the wonderful technology that we are all here to talk about.

Fear. Fear can be a good emotion. Fear can help us be more pragmatic. Fear can hold us in check. Fear can allow us to think clearly about the strategies that we must use to be successful. But fear as well can hold us back. Fear of failure. Fear of making a mistake. Fear of the unknown. Fear of taking risks. This kind of fear can paralyze us. Can cause companies to stop when they should go forward.

Desire. Desire can be a wonderful motivator to act. It can cause us to do things boldly, with imagination, with courage. It can cause us to make choices that we would otherwise not be prepared to make. And yet, there are some things about desire that also one must be careful of. And frankly, we see some of the downside of desire today in many dot.com companies. Too much desire can turn into destructive greed. Too much desire can blind us to strategy, to pragmatism, to reality. Because without the tempering of reality, desire can make us too impulsive. And in this impulsiveness, we can risk alienating our partners. We can exhaust our employees. We can disappoint our shareowners.

Too much fear and companies become paralyzed by uncertainty and doubt. Too much desire and they flame out. And so I believe how we choose between fear and desire will motivate us and will help determine our success in this new economy.

The best course of action, I believe, is to have an honest assessment of both our deepest fears and our most fervent desires. The most successful companies, I believe, will harness the power of both their fear and their desire. To fuel our best thinking, to energize our ranks and to leapfrog the competition.

Which brings us back, perhaps, to the spirit of inventiveness. Truly inventive businesses will use the power of both fear and desire as a motivation to how they approach the net economy. Inventive companies will embrace their deepest fears. And they will look at these fears to help them make rational decisions, to get the best balance from dot.com agility and brick-and-mortar stability. And they will use the combination of fear and desire to forge their best partnerships. They will harness their intense desires. Desire to be first, the desire to further human progress, the desire to make money in new ways. To set the course for the next wave of business in the new economy.[16]

ESCAPE FROM S-CATRAZ

Now that we have become acquainted with the black knights – the friends of success and at the same time the enemies of renewal – it is time to learn about the weapons we can use in our battle against them. These weapons are closely related to the themes discussed by Fiorina: fear and desire. The S-curves are older than humanity. It is thus hardly surprising that we all have weapons in our nature that can prevent us hanging on to a dying S-curve. These weapons are our own survival instincts. These survival instincts, attachment and exploration, govern to a large degree how we approach the conservation of the "now" – or renewal and the exploration of the unknown future. The evolution and nature of these instincts is the subject of the next chapter, in which we explain the way they work. In the chapters following, we look at what is required to help these omnipresent human powers come into flower within an organization.

2. *Attachment and Exploration*

The ability to accept challenge…is locked in the human DNA.
Carly Fiorina, former president and CEO of Hewlett-Packard

Each living creature is also a fossil. It carries within itself, right down to the microscopic structure of its proteins, the traces and even the blemishes of its ancestors. This is even truer for the human than for any other animal because of the dual evolution – physical and mental – that he has inherited.
Jacques Monod[1]

What the genes determine is not necessarily one single behavior, but rather the ability to develop certain behaviors and, what is even more important, the tendency to demonstrate them in a variety of specific environments.
Edward Wilson[2]

E VERYBODY, even those in an organization who are eager for renewal, will fall into "Escher's trap" (see Chapter 1) and end up in S-catraz. Everybody is naturally inclined to adopt yesterday's success strategy in the hope and expectation that it can prove useful for a little while longer.

At the end of the previous chapter, I suggested that one of the most important tasks of a manager is to keep a watchful eye on the way the different S-curves develop and to support the organization in its jump from one S-curve to another. I have noticed that such jumps are always accompanied by fear of the unknown; fear of the loss of all that is familiar and trusted; and hope in the future. In this chapter, we look at the way in which people, for many million years, have handled their fear of leaving the familiar and at their hope of improvement. We shall see how human behavior is governed in both familiar and unfamiliar situations by instinctive systems: the *attachment system* and the *exploration system*.

It can be interesting for managers to understand the attachment and exploration systems. Insight into these instincts is, in fact, one of the keys to escaping from S-catraz and creating the parameters within which an alert, flexible, and constantly innovating organization can develop.

"Modern society" is several hundred years or, depending on the definition, 10,000–15,000 years old. Approximately 15,000 years ago, we drastically changed our way of life when we discovered agriculture: We began living in one place, in gradually larger groups. Before that time, we had spent millions of years living the lives of nomads in small groups of 10–100 individuals. The era in which we live in the same place with larger groups of people is – in the context of evolution – far too short to have left any discernible traces on our physical and instinctive characteristics. We are almost precisely the same people as the farmers who lived in the Low Countries some 2,000 years ago and the nomads who, 10,000 and even 100,000 years ago, roamed across the steppes. What is more, an important part of our behavior finds its origin in the evolution of the mammals some 200 million years ago.[3]

ETHOLOGY: A NEW SOURCE OF INSPIRATION FOR MANAGEMENT

It is remarkable that the behavior of people in organizations has seldom been discussed in management literature in any systematic way from a biological or evolutionary perspective. Yet ethology offers insights into human behavior that could prove invaluable for managers in the current situation. Ethology is based on the conviction that behavioral systems have evolved through natural selection and that the basis for the behavior we see today was laid down millions of years ago. In other words, it is not only the *external characteristics* of humans and animals (color of eyes or skin) that have an evolutionary background: Many aspects of *behavior* can also be understood from evolutionary development. Ethology makes use of the cybernetic principles of feedforward and feedback that I outlined in Chapter 1. Konrad Lorenz, Nikolaas Tinbergen, and Robert Hinde are all scientists who have conducted research – into both attachment and exploration – from an ethological perspective. John Bowlby approached attachment from the viewpoint of psychoanalysis.[4] He did this by combining psychoanalytical principles with those of ethology and cybernetics, as researched by the scientists mentioned. For Bowlby, *attachment* was first and foremost the bonding of a child with its parents. As we shall see later, attachment covers a very wide area indeed.

Evolution has given us a body with survival instincts and a repertoire of behavior that we can use to aid those survival instincts. Two of these survival instincts are particularly relevant to understanding the behavior of organizations: *attachment* and *exploration*. A good understanding of these two instincts, or behavior patterns, will help managers understand on a

36

much deeper level the change processes within an organization. Insight into attachment and exploration helps managers understand what motivates people to act in a certain way. When managers understand the mechanics of attachment and exploration, they have the most important keys in their hands for helping their organization escape from S-catraz.

Attachment and exploration are two instinctive systems that, in the course of millions of years, have contributed to the survival and development of what finally evolved into the human species. The attachment instinct is primarily directed at safety. Attachment also creates the conditions for knowledge exchange. But the very fact that attachment can create strong bonds within groups could, within the environment of evolutionary adaptation, create a threatening situation. After all, chances, possibilities, sources of food and water, and possible escape routes were all *outside* the group. If the group did not look outside itself, then there was little chance of it surviving. The exploration system seems to provide an answer to this: an instinct that directs itself at everything that is new, that was previously unknown, and that generally exists outside the immediate environment.

The basic instincts of attachment and exploration are readily observed in children, and the following example will make this very clear. This example shows how attachment and exploration go hand in hand and alternate with each other.

ILLUSTRATION OF THE ATTACHMENT AND EXPLORATION SYSTEMS: A GARDEN PARTY ON A SUNDAY AFTERNOON

Just imagine that you have been invited to a garden party, with your partner and your four-year-old child, on a warm, sunny Sunday afternoon. Right from the moment you arrive, you enjoy yourself. There are a lot of people there, there is plenty of food and drink, and there is also a group of children playing with each other – running happily backward and forward through the patio doors. You know the house and many of the guests quite well: After all, you are visiting your very good friends. But your child, on the other hand, is just four, has never been here before and doesn't know any of the children or grown-ups. For the child, everything is new and unfamiliar. When you arrive, the three of you stand in the entrance hall, where the sounds from the living room and the garden can already be clearly heard. Then suddenly the door opens, your friends immediately recognize you and come to greet you. The sounds become loud; it is the sound of the children playing together.

"What does your child do at that moment?" Answer: It stands as close to you as possible and may even grab hold of you. This reaction is a type of behavior driven by the attachment system. There are, of course, other types of reaction: Some children may cling even more tightly to their parents, others slightly less. Some children notice a toy that reminds them of something they have at home, and immediately go to it and start playing with it. Most children, however, will grab hold of their parents; we will explore this action further.

"What happens if you try to push your child away from you in the direction of the other children?" The majority of children will then grab their parents even more tightly. The more you try to push your child away, the more tightly it grabs you.

"Does it help if you try to explain to your child that there is no reason to be scared?" No, it doesn't help. You will probably be unable to think of any similar situation in which a child will be persuaded by arguments. This doesn't mean that it never happens – but it would then be the exception that proves the proverbial rule. This brings us to the next question.

"What, then, do you do as parents?" You take your time. You keep your child near you, let it sit on your lap, or even allow it to hide, literally, under its mother's skirt. You don't really have any choice.

"What does your child do if you keep it near you, on your lap, or standing in your shadow?" Once again, most people will give the same answer: It will gradually start looking around inquisitively – it will start *exploring*. It starts peeping around and, gradually, will become increasingly curious. After a while, the curiosity will become too much for the child, and it will carefully start scouting the new environment and people, until it is finally fully absorbed into the group of children, where it learns new things, plays, becomes enthusiastic, and… apparently forgets all about its parents. In fact, the child may actually object to any interference from its parents. The child that, just a while ago, would not venture even half a step from its parents suddenly indicates – with the same stubbornness – that it is perfectly capable of looking after itself.

"Will you no longer be able to notice the relationship between child and parents?" Certainly. The child sometimes looks around at its parents. Sometimes comes to say hello. Brings something to show them. If you left without saying anything and the child noticed, it would immediately

become uneasy; then, even the slightest event would be enough to scare or panic the child: end of exploration. And now the last question about this situation.

"*What happens when you want to go home?*" The child is often reluctant to leave the environment that, initially, it wouldn't explore on its own.

This example of a child at a garden party shows in a nutshell the dynamics of attachment and exploration. The initial behavior that we recognize in the child in a strange situation is its tendency to stay close to its parents and even hang on to them. If the parents try to force the child to play with the other children, the child will hang on even more tightly to its parents. The child thinks the situation is too dangerous, too unknown to start exploring. Looking to parents for security is behavior that is triggered by the attachment system. When the child feels more secure in the environment, then the exploratory behavior comes into play: Slowly scouting, then investigating, and finally becoming part of the environment is behavior triggered by the exploration system. While the child plays, it occasionally checks where its parents are. This behavior is triggered by the attachment system that sometimes – while exploration is taking place – carries out a (feedback) check.

ABOUT ATTACHMENT

Attachment – which can also mean "bonding" – is organized as a feedback system. The attachment system is intended to maintain stable bonded relationships. These bonded relationships ensured, in prehistoric times, that the group stayed together, that people were less vulnerable, and – an additional benefit – that they could exchange knowledge.

In the garden party example, we saw that the child regarded its parents as its source of security. It is clear in this example that there is a strong bond, clearly directed at people, that is apparently activated by something such as an unknown environment. The child has its own norm: "*Those people (in this case its parents) are my refuge and home base.*" This norm determines the behavior of the child in the various situations described in the example.

Later on in life, this norm is extended. We no longer feel attached just to our mother and father, nor do we look exclusively to them for our feeling of security. Attachment can be (and in most cases is) directed at others, such as brothers and sisters, partners, and colleagues.

Attachment does not appear to have a single uniform strength, but rather runs the gamut from very weak to very strong. In addition (and here I am getting ahead of myself by mentioning the *differences* in attachment that I deal with in Chapter 4), attachment can be less directed at people and more at other matters, such as techniques or concepts.

As we get older, there is also a change in the *manner* in which we determine the presence of those to whom we are attached. In the garden party example, the parents of the child have to be – literally – in sight. The child does not allow the distance to become greater than a few feet. As people get older, this process becomes much more abstract. As adults, we no longer need our friends constantly near us. It can be sufficient that we are aware of each other's existence, and that we are able to contact each other by telephone or email when we are in need of support or when we wish to share something.

ABOUT EXPLORATION

The child at the garden party decides, at a certain moment, that it is sufficiently accustomed to the environment and should explore it further. *Exploration* is a general term used by ethologists to indicate the "scouting" side of humans: playing, being curious, being motivated to try out new things.

This exploratory side of humans has not, if we look at history, been completely useless. In current technological developments, the competitive advantage of exploration seems to have become ever stronger. Exploratory behavior is derived from an interest in the unknown, without initially caring whether it will result in any advantage or not. This last remark is crucial for a full understanding of exploration. Exploration is curiosity for anything new. People who have been able to retain their exploratory behavior into adulthood, and to develop it further, are seldom bothered by the top of the S-curve with all its stabilizing feedback. Instinctively, they look for new ideas that can result in new S-curves.

In ethology, one question has been around for some time: "Is exploration a separate instinctive system?"

Archer and Birke have summarized a lot of research into exploration. They realized that psychology initially found it difficult to recognize exploration as a separate system. After all, the classic motivation theories were constructed on feedback systems. Somebody takes a glass of water in order to replenish a deficit of moisture. In other words, exploration seems to be the *only* human instinct that does *not* have the characteristics of a feedback system. Archer and Birke mention in this context that "exploration has not played any significant role in the debate about motivation systems, largely because it does not fit comfortably into the classic theory concerning human instincts."[5]

The child at the garden party is (we assume) neither hungry nor thirsty and doesn't need to use the bathroom, but instead (once the environment feels sufficiently safe) goes intuitively to something that just happens to attract its attention.

If *exploratory behavior* is defined as "all activities aimed at gathering information about the environment," then satisfying any need contains a certain degree of exploratory behavior. If the child at the garden party wants to use the bathroom, then it will make use of information from the environment. That gathering of information, however, is clearly at the service of satisfying an acute need. Ethologists therefore make a distinction between *extrinsic exploration* and *intrinsic exploration*.[6] *Extrinsic exploration* is exploratory behavior that is intended to obtain information that can contribute to the satisfaction of a personal need for food, drink, social contact, and so on; this sort of exploratory behavior is put to the service of something other than looking for a completely new idea. *Intrinsic exploration* is specifically aimed at obtaining information from the environment and is specifically activated by triggers from the environment – in other words, "searching for change when (and simply and only because) the existing has become too common." This is all about exploration for the sake of exploration, setting off into the unknown just for the fun of it. It is all about fundamental exploration, rather than applied exploration – and this is the type of exploration that companies need most in the current turbulent world.

It wasn't until the 1950s, when ethologists understood the difference between intrinsic and extrinsic exploration, that exploration became accepted as a separate human motive. In this book, we use *exploration* to refer to "intrinsic exploration." The following quotation from Archer and Birke explains *intrinsic exploration* in other terms: "Exploration is considered the process that an animal uses to obtain knowledge about its environment, so that it can function within that environment…The most important advantage of solid knowledge of the surroundings is that the animal can adapt its survival strategies accordingly."[7]

Lorenz too considers exploration a separate motive that can only operate if the surroundings are free of "tension." Lorenz adds that the exploration motive is no weaker than any other motive. The motivation for exploration can be stronger than hunger or danger, and, says Lorenz, this is well illustrated by the saying "curiosity killed the cat." In this, the exploration motive differentiates itself from the other human motives such as our need for food and drink, sex or sleep, power or territory, acceptance or security. Lorenz: "Exploratory behavior is different from all the other 'normal' motives and obtains the sort of information that can be called objective in exactly the same way as results from scientific research undertaken by people."[8]

EXPLORATORY AND STABILITY-CENTERED PEOPLE

In practice, congenital, acquired, and cultural factors together influence the degree to which a person is more or less exploratory or more or less stability-centered. Some people are more exploratory than others. Some people feel comfortable in a set of established structures and existing rules, and feel little need to bring any change to this situation. They derive considerable satisfaction from further improving that which already exists. For others, the exploratory urge is so strong that they constantly set out along un-known paths, taking the possibility of failure in their stride. They are, deep in their hearts, just as scared of the unknown as anybody else, but the urge to discover and experience new things is stronger than their fear. There are people who are extremely exploratory and others who are extremely stability-centered. Most people are somewhere between these two extremes. Apparently, there is a "normal" distribution along the scale: Only a very few people are either *extremely* exploratory or *extremely* stability-centered; a larger proportion is *highly* exploratory or *highly* stability-centered; and the greater proportion is somewhere in the middle – they are *slightly* explora-tory or *slightly* stability-centered. *Exploratory people* can also be called "explorers of the new"; *stability-centered people* can be called "conservers of the good."

These differences can arise from a combination of congenital, acquired, and contextual factors.

1 *The congenital factor.* It seems obvious that a number of factors in the balance between an exploratory attitude and a stability-centered attitude can be attributed to congenital factors.
2 *The acquired factor.* Nurture and life experience have naturally also had a meaningful impact on the way in which human beings are formed. The degree of safe attachment in youth has undoubtedly a significant

influence, as the research of Mary Ainsworth and others has demonstrated, but this is equally true of the degree to which certain attitudes and behavior are rewarded or denied during youth.

3 *The contextual factor.* People can reach the conclusion that exploratory behavior is not valued in the organization where they work. They see what has happened to colleagues who have proposed something new and unusual that did not become a success: They have lost faith in the organization, or "their mistake" has dogged them for years to come. No matter how loudly the management of such an organization proclaims that initiatives are valued and that employees are allowed to make mistakes, one single example that proves the opposite is enough to see exploration banished from the stage. There are organizations where exploratory behavior is actively encouraged, where initiatives are rewarded, and where people who are prepared to take risks are highly valued. In such organizations, mistakes and failures are seen as an inevitable by-product of success. In such an organization, people feel stimulated to explore unfamiliar paths and to use their exploratory powers to the full.

ATTACHMENT AND EXPLORATION ARE AT THE VERY ROOT OF AN ORGANIZATION'S POTENTIAL FOR CHANGE

Exploratory people, who feel at home in unknown, unstructured situations that demand improvisational talent, will also feel comfortable at the start of the S-curve, in the pioneering stage of an organization. Those who feel at home in existing structures will feel comfortable in the upper regions of the S-curve, where consolidation and efficiency are important.

The reason it is so difficult to bring about major change in organizations is twofold. Often, such major changes take place at the end of the S-curve. If we look at large organizations that have worked in a certain way for some time, then we will find that the original pioneers have long since left and that stability-centered people are now in the majority. This is fine if we are talking about making full use of the possibilities offered by the old S-curve. The resistance to change is at its strongest, and there is little or no forward push towards a new and unknown future. I will return to this aspect of *diversity* in Chapter 6.

The organization of innovation and self-preservation in our minds

As evolution progressed, so an additional layer of brain cells was added over our primeval instincts: We call these the *neocortex* or *cortex*. In the schematic drawings opposite, the old brain is in the middle and the new brain is wrapped around it. Our survival instincts are rooted in the old brain, but our thought processes are made possible by the new brain. These new layers of brain cells were responsible for our enormous competitive advantage. All mammals have a neocortex, but that of man is by far the most developed. This highly developed neocortex gives us our ability for language and our awareness of time, but it also gives us our ability to think associatively: to make links, to see chaos and patterns. This ability has allowed humans to adapt faster and more intelligently to their surroundings.

Our brain cortex seems to have been intended originally to satisfy existing basic needs with even greater intelligence. If you could think up cleverer ways of finding food, defending territory, and forming stronger groups, then you had a better chance of survival. From an evolutionary perspective, the cortex has used its competencies for millions of years to achieve the same ends. The exploration system is therefore essential for survival.

But what happens if the associative cortex is no longer directed by the basic feedback-oriented urge for survival from the old brain? Just imagine there is no thirst, no hunger, no sexual desire; there is no need to defend any territory or to determine the pecking order in the group; and there is no need to secure attachment. Well, that leaves a freely associative cortex in which information can freely find its way. I can imagine that the first cave drawings found their origins here: All at once, there is sufficient time and tranquility to allow the mind to play freely with the images of the world and to discover whatever there is to discover. A feed-forward-driven process emerges, and new information is formed by the associated images that organize themselves in the cortex. If you can view the world without being concerned about your own survival (whether that is your own physical survival or the survival of an organization), then your curiosity about the world will have free rein. Then the enormous creative power of the neocortex can be used for creating, discovering, exploring, and innovating. As mentioned, the figures here are simple representations – undoubtedly ones that do little justice to the real complexity – of the principle we have just discussed.

In Figure 2.1, the old brains are represented by the oval shape in the middle. The new associative brains (which also make connections) are illustrated as a covering around the old brains. The illustration on the left shows how observation is directed by the old brains. The old brains judge the information they

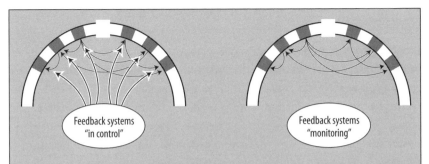

Feedback systems "in control"

Feedback systems "monitoring"

Figure 2.1 *The relationship between "old" and "new" brains*

receive from outside for its usefulness in terms of direct survival. The system in the old brains constantly asks itself: "Can I use this information to satisfy a basic need? If I can, I will use this information; if I can't, I will ignore it." The illustration on the right shows that the old brains do not have any control over the new brains: The information does not need to satisfy any basic need. The neocortex has the space to take the information it receives from the outside world at face value.

In Figure 2.2, we show the communication between three people. These people pass information on to each other. In the top row, the communication takes place in an environment of unsafe attachment, and this causes the content to be adapted quickly to each person's own political needs, and shows a decline. In the bottom row, where information is passed on in a safely attached environment, this decline hardly occurs.

When people work together, this effect is magnified: The less people have to think about survival, the less interference there is to the information and the stronger the creative process can become.

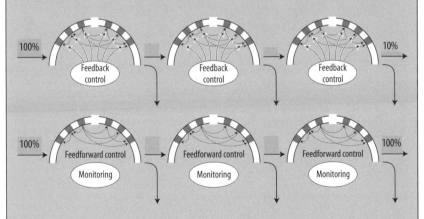

Figure 2.2 *The attachment system influences the "interference" in information*

45

If people feel safely attached in an organization, they will tend to concentrate their energies on the outside world and on those things that are necessary for reacting creatively and constructively to that outside world. If they feel insecure, they will direct all their energy towards creating a safe home base. The result is that people concentrate on internal matters, devoting their energy to power struggles, or become passive, simply following orders. Exploration is the only instinct that can help us escape "Escher's trap." Exploration is the drive to change before the outside world changes. Change can, of course, take place in an organization without exploration, but then the change is forced on the organization by external events, such as a possible bankruptcy, a company takeover, or drastic downsizing.

Exploratory behavior is not better than stability-centered behavior. Feedforward thinking is not better than feedback thinking. Both orientations are necessary if the S-curve in an organization is to be navigated with success. But if a secure environment is missing, then attachment remains but exploration disappears. The next chapter looks at how the leadership of an organization can create a climate in which both attachment and exploration can flourish. This can result in an organization that is both efficient and stable, but at the same time able to react alertly, creatively, and innovatively to changes in the environment.

3. *Inconsistency: The Assassin of Changeability*

Leadership motivates people by satisfying fundamental human needs.
J. P. Kotter[1]

MANAGERS do not get exploration in their organizations as a gift. One of the most important tasks in the management of an organization is to ensure a climate in which people feel safely enough attached to be able to explore. This whole book considerably simplifies the ethological aspects, and that in itself is dangerous. One of those risks involves the term *safely attached*. *Safe* does not, in this context, mean that there is no danger for the organization or that there is no competition from outside or that there is no threat from fundamental structural change (takeovers, reorganizations, and so on). Safe attachment has to do with underlying relationships. It is precisely safe attachment that makes it possible for people to tackle very risky situations together. If, within an organization, there is a culture of unsafe attachment, then the tendency is to turn the attention away from external risks, rather than to explore them innovatively.

In this chapter I will look at what *safe attachment* actually means in the area of management and organization. How can the top of an organization create a climate in which exploration can flourish?

All sorts of seemingly innocent management behavior can damage the climate of security, and thus reduce the organization's ability to change. This management behavior can be defined, simply, as "inconsistency." Inconsistency is the assassin: It is just as dangerous for the changeability of an organization as smoking is for health. It does its work invisibly and lethally (what difference does that one cigarette make?). It doesn't really seem to make much difference if you miss that one appointment; if, just for once, you don't do what you promised, aren't totally open about your intentions, or put off decisions about awkward dilemmas. Many managers will say, "What is so dangerous about preaching the need for personal development and attention, but not being able to find the time to hold assessment discussions with my employees? Surely a manager must be allowed to set a bad example once in a while. After all, I'm only human."

And they'd be right – a manager is only human. Nevertheless, inconsistency in a manager is unforgivable. All those examples of inconsistency – a badly prepared assessment meeting, not keeping appointments, saying one thing and doing another – are only *seemingly* innocent. The way in which people react to the inconsistency they experience in their direct surroundings is actually biologically determined: It has been engraved over millions of years on our genetic material.

This chapter deals with the instinctive reaction of people – every single one of us, without exception – which explains why inconsistency is the greatest spell-breaker in organizations. But first we have to examine the term *consistency*. What is consistency? And why is it so difficult to be consistent?

WHAT IS CONSISTENCY?

The *Oxford English Dictionary* defines *consistency* as "the quality, state, or fact of being consistent; agreement, harmony, compatibility (with something, of things, or of one thing with another)." The degree to which somebody is consistent cannot be judged by incidental behavior. Consistency is a *pattern* that becomes apparent from a collection of actions over a longer period of time.[2] But how can we act consistently? After all, the rapid changes around us mean that we have to be flexible. A long-term strategy is virtually a thing of the past. Nevertheless, there are a number of "beacons" and "anchor points" for consistent behavior. One such beacon can be the organization's mission, or the vision an organization has about its own existence, or the values that the organization represents. When an organization acts and makes decisions in line with its mission, its aims or values, then consistency is created for the employees. They know what they can expect from management. They also know what is expected of them when they take decisions themselves. Such consistent behavior creates a calm and transparent environment, even in the most hectic circumstances.

Most books about leadership examine consistency from many different sides. Sometimes, the word *consistency* is not even used. Take, for example, the following remark by Thomas Peters and Robert Waterman at the end of *In Search of Excellence* from 1982: "But so many can't see it. There are always practical, justifiable, sensible, and sane reasons to compromise on any of these variables. Only those simplistic people – such as Watson, Hewlett, Packard, Kroc, Mars, Olsen, McPherson, Marriott, Procter, Gamble, Johnson – stayed simplistic. And their companies remarkably successful."[3]

A decade after Peters and Waterman, Collins and Porras did research at the University of Stanford into the power of consistency in corporate life. They looked for the factors that determined the difference between organizations that had, over a longer period of time, functioned *well* and those that had, over the same period, functioned *excellently*. The main thrust of their work, published in the famous book *Built to Last*, is that the best organizations that have the ability to reinvent themselves (for decades in succession) all have one thing in common: consistency or alignment – in other words, maintaining and protecting the core values and core purpose. In *Built to Last* – sometimes called "the *In Search of Excellence* of the 1990s" – they write: "And the best organizations, wherever they are, pay considerable attention to consistency and alignment."[4]

Joseph Badaracco of Harvard Business School shows that leaders can gain the trust of their organizations if those leaders' personal behavior demonstrates – day after day – that they are people of integrity, and shows that they put into practice the mission, values, and aspirations of the organization.[5]

Another example: Stephen Covey writes in *The Seven Habits of Highly Effective People* that "your certainty is based on the correct principles, regardless of the external situation or circumstances."[6] Here Covey shows that *consistency* is not the same as "always reacting in the same way." Take, for example, the idea that you should always keep appointments. Nobody really questions this. But just suppose that you have a boss who always, without fail, keeps his appointments with you. Imagine, just for a moment, that one day your boss turns up on time for a routine work progress meeting. Afterwards, you learn that a colleague had asked your boss to drive him to the hospital where his wife had just gone into labor. Your boss refused because he had an appointment with you – and appointments are there to be kept. If you get to know about this, then you probably won't think of your boss as more reliable – probably you'll think just the reverse.

Somebody who, in my opinion, has best described what I mean here is Joseph Badaracco in his book *Leadership and the Quest for Integrity*: "Consistency does not mean that decision-making and managing are forced into a straitjacket or subject to strict rules and regulations. A manager has to adapt his actions to circumstances…Consistency means that personal values and organizational aims will largely dictate what a manager does and says. Integrity in the way a manager acts means that the rules may not be changed."[7] That is, somebody who, to use the words of Covey quoted above, always *acts* in the same way under every set of circumstances is not consistent but dogmatic. This is why Covey's remark about "correct principles" is so important. It is all about being consistent in the application of values and aims. This is not the same as always showing the same behavior.

The increasing emphasis placed in management literature on the importance of consistency is hardly surprising: Inconsistency is everywhere. In our society we receive information about specific subjects from a wide variety of sources. For example, I can watch both CNN and al-Jazeera for news about the Middle East. Thanks to this "redundancy" in the information stream, inconsistencies that were unapparent 10 or 20 years ago are now increasingly highlighted. Not only is inconsistency apparent, but, because of our increasing awareness, we also notice it more easily; we have become more critical and reach conclusions more quickly.

Although most people recognize the importance of consistency, inconsistency in organizations seems to be the rule rather than the exception. This has, in my opinion, two causes. First, it is difficult to be consistent: It demands a constant and conscious investment in terms of time, attention, and discipline in order to maintain consistency. And second, the danger of inconsistency is underestimated.

BEING CONSISTENT DEMANDS CONSTANT ATTENTION AND DISCIPLINE

Managers are constantly confronted with all sorts of large and small problems, and people expect them to take decisions or to give their opinions about them. In order to be consistent, managers must have a very clear understanding of their personal values and personal aims. What are the sources of energy and pleasure? What borders may not be crossed without damaging personal integrity? What things make life worth while? A clear understanding of personal values and aims means that managers can constantly use them as a sounding board for their actions. It requires attention and discipline to make use of this sounding board. It will lead to awkward discussions; and such an attitude will not make it any easier to solve the dilemmas that commonly confront people. It also requires a certain skill to act in accordance with personal values and aims without turning into some latter-day Don Quixote tilting at windmills in the organization. Badaracco describes in his book *Defining Moments: When Managers Must Choose between Right and Right* how things such as timing, and insight into the interests of other parties in the organization, play a role in the consistency and effectiveness of managers.[8]

If consistency is to be achieved in an organization, then it is not enough that individual managers use their own values and aims as a sounding board. The organization *as a whole* also has its own values and aims. We are not talking here about the values and aims that it says it has, but rather about those that it demonstrates in its day-to-day activities. These values cannot be thought up during a "day in the country": They can be uncovered by taking a long, hard look at what is already there. Similarly, the core aims of an organization cannot be simply changed from day to day according to the direction of the wind: These core aims are an integral part of an organization's identity. The values and core aims of an organization cannot and need not match one hundred percent those of the individuals that work there. Problems arise, however, when there is *no overlap at all*: The result is constant conflicts about fundamental matters – or the people in question come into conflict with themselves, with all the consequences of stress and lack of motivation.

It is difficult enough for an individual manager to be consistent. For a team it is much more difficult to act consistently with those around it. A number of things are essential if a team is to operate consistently: consensus about values, the dream, the vision, and the mission (the top of the feedforward hierarchy); open feedback about the way each member acts in the team; and careful handling of communications.

Consistency demands consensus about values, dream, vision, and mission
The top of the feedforward hierarchy (see Chapter 1, Figure 1.6), which forms the foundation of the organization, is the most important source of consistency. Yet these subjects are rarely discussed in any depth at board meetings. Even rarer are board meetings where the members openly discuss personal views regarding values, the dream that people are trying to realize, the vision of the future, and the mission of the organization. Often people assume differences of opinion about these matters, but these are seldom addressed openly. Everybody does their own thing – for better or for worse – in the assumption that it doesn't really make any difference one way or another. It is, however, of fundamental importance that board members tackle their differences and carry on until they reach a consensus about the mission – based on a consensus about values, dream, and vision – and one that is supported without any reservations by every single member. Even the smallest difference of opinion about this among board members is enough to sow confusion throughout the organization. The lower you go in the organization, the more these differences are magnified, and the

greater the interference and the lack of clarity about frameworks, aims, and rules become.

Consistency demands open feedback

Consistency is not an isolated action or a regular pattern of behavior, but a process of mutual interaction. In my consultancy it has become clear that about 70% of managers have at least one fundamental blind spot.[9] The following are fairly commonplace.

- People consider themselves to be exceptionally exploratory, while everybody around them thinks they are highly stability-oriented.
- People consider themselves to be very people-oriented and supportive, but the opinion of those around them is that they are very confrontational and hungry for power.

Such blind spots cause interference. Good intentions have a way of rebounding: Behavior that is meant to be consistent and well intentioned is experienced as unreliable behavior. If these blind spots are to be defused, then the leadership will have to ask for feedback; such feedback becomes even more valuable when the members of the management team discuss the information – and therefore the blind spots – openly and frankly with each other. Most people don't find this easy, because it means you have to admit your vulnerability. But if such a discussion can be held, under the direction of a reliable discussion leader, then the team will profit from increased trust between its members, and the team will be more consistent towards the organization as a whole. These benefits are attainable by everybody who wants to act consistently but is unaware of the dangers of inconsistency. That is, the vast majority of people. Individual leaders and managers who use inconsistency more or less intentionally as a management instrument for generating fear are in a class of their own.

Consistency demands careful handling of communications

Inconsistency can also arise in a management team that has achieved the underlying trust essential for consistency but is not careful about communications. Even somebody who is determined to be open in all communications will still need to handle things carefully. The ease with which inconsistency arises is demonstrated by a test that my colleagues and I use at the close of strategic management conferences. Depending on the content, such conferences generally last for one to three days. Quite often, a team can come under time pressure for the duration. This can be because certain underlying conflicts have gone unresolved, but also because of enthusiasm or deep involvement with the material. During such strategy meetings, my colleagues and I often become involved to ensure that the processes can be finished with a quality result in the time available. It is hardly surprising that these extremely busy managers look up in surprise when we suggest that of the two days that they have left for handling matters, they should devote one-quarter of the time (the last afternoon) to thinking about how to communicate the results to the rest of the organization. In the final afternoon session, the managers try to imagine how, the next morning, they will communicate to the members of the teams that they each lead the decisions that have been taken. Their assignment is as follows: The participants prepare for the situation in which, the following morning, they will report to their teams the results of the meeting. This practical solution is then simulated. Each participant is allotted five minutes to show how they will communicate the results of the meeting. The remaining participants assume the role of the team members in the simulated situation. In general, the participants are sufficiently acquainted with each other's subordinates. It comes as a surprise to the team how easily they can assume a certain role, and how sharply the group is able to detect, thanks to this role-play, unspoken inconsistencies and lack of clarity.

This proves to a team that, if the exercise had not been undertaken, the team would have continued with these inconsistencies, and that these inconsistencies – regardless of all good intentions – would have led to confusion in the organization. The exercise also clearly proves that knowledge about the inconsistencies was already available in the team. A team that underestimates the importance of consistency and avoids potentially deep and lively conflicts will never be able to make use of this knowledge. The inconsistency that thus remains buried in the team will later be magnified in the organization and continue its divisive work. It is exactly this magnification of inconsistency that is dealt with in Chapter 7, where we discuss its place in the policy of an organization and how an organization that wishes to explore (innovate) will have to operate in the area of internal communications.

THE DANGER OF INCONSISTENCY IS UNDERESTIMATED

Inconsistent, unpredictable behavior is dangerous for organizations. You don't even have to go into an organization to realize how dangerous inconsistency is – and how insidiously it can creep in. Just look at what happens when parents are inconsistent in the way they raise their children. Generally, children are masters at detecting inconsistencies. What happens if parents send inconsistent signals to their children about essential things such as homework, performance, honesty, respect, keeping to agreements, and such like? If parents have different views on such matters and react differently to them, then the results they achieve are often cynical children who play off one parent against the other and who manipulate them. A specific example: smoking. Whether a child takes up smoking or not is, statistically speaking, largely determined by the smoking habits of its parents. If the parents smoke, then there is virtually no reward or punishment that will help prevent the children from smoking. As we have said, inconsistency in parental behavior is rewarded by manipulation on the part of the children. When parents act inconsistently, children lose their bearings. A child will start feeling insecure – even if this goes unnoticed. The child loses the security and clarity it needs to be able to explore. Manipulation is a form of control and power, and thus one of the "strategies" a child uses to regain lost feelings of security.

When the management of an organization is inconsistent, the same thing happens: Employees feel that they do not have a good grip on the situation. They start feeling insecure and begin developing "survival strategies." They start looking for ways to control the situation themselves: If they get the feeling that they cannot trust management, then they want to be able to trust themselves and their direct colleagues. They concentrate on self-preservation.

In an organization where inconsistency rules at the top, the weeds of opportunistic politics will flourish. Look around you, in your own organization, and see just how carelessly people communicate with each other. How often do you leave a meeting without first making clear decisions about what must happen next? How often are appointments not kept, without any consequences being associated with that? Managers who allow this to happen are paid back with employees (and colleagues) who follow their own road maps, play off managers one against the other, and engage in manipulation. The dynamics in such an organization differ little from those in a family where the parents are inconsistent.

CONSISTENCY AND INCONSISTENCY ARE POWERFUL SIGNALS TO OUR ATTACHMENT SYSTEM

The strength of the signal inconsistency gives to our attachment system can be seen if we go back to the time when the instincts of humans (or their immediate ancestors) were formed. That time lies far in the memory of our species: long before the emergence of *Homo sapiens* 300,000 or 400,000 years ago, and perhaps even further back than the emergence of the first apelike creatures more than 5 million years ago. Complex genetic changes require a lot of time. In light of the long evolution of man, even the first primitive agricultural communities (10,000–12,000 years ago) were, in a way, just yesterday. The modern organizational forms that were formed 200 years ago, during the Industrial Revolution, are, in such a context, not past at all. In hundreds of thousands of years, there has been no real change in the genetic basis for attachment or exploration.

If we are to understand attachment and exploration, then we have to look at the environment in which our "instincts" made a maximum contribution to the survival of the human species. Our ancestors lived in groups of 100 at the most. A group of that size was sufficiently large to offer protection, and sufficiently small and flexible enough to move quickly from one place to another. Dangers included predators and lack of food. Our exploration system evolved because we had to seek our survival in our surroundings. Our exploration instinct is attracted by everything that is new and unknown. It first wants to explore, and then to make a judgment. But anything you don't know could be dangerous. And so our ancestors were faced with a dilemma: If they didn't go and investigate, then that would mean, sooner or later, the end; if they did go, then it could mean danger. In practice, the choice was easily made: Not going out to explore was not an option. Danger had to be accepted. The chance of danger had, of course, to be minimized, but was nevertheless accepted. There was – and is – a constant interaction between our attachment system and our exploration system. What exactly would it take for one of our ancestors to abandon the exploration and return to the group?

One answer could be: when they encountered a predator. Stone Age man saw danger, became scared (the attachment system was stimulated into action), and ran back to the group. In that case, those ancestors who could run back to the group quickly enough would survive. But we know that many predators could run a lot faster than our ancestors. And so it was often the case that more than one person was exploring at the same time; the one that could run faster would survive. Sorry about the less athletic ancestor – but, hey, it's survival of the fittest, right? In that case, the human species would have evolved into a highly specialized athlete with long, muscular legs. This has happened in the animal kingdom – just look at antelopes and zebras. In order to survive, they move around in groups and they are very good at galloping. But by specializing "themselves" in this way, these animals have become rather one-sided. The human species, however, survived thanks to its versatility and ingenuity, and doesn't really impress in its sprinting abilities. We have to take a different road if we are to explain how our genetic ancestors solved this or, to be more precise, how evolution solved this. In other words, how has evolution programmed us so that we can explore without running such great risks that our adventure will be rewarded with death?

OUR SURVIVAL STRATEGY: BETTER SAFE THAN SORRY

The survival solution that has evolved in the human species is, in essence, a combination of statistics and natural selection. It is "better safe than sorry" – perhaps not the most courageous and heroic variant of survival, but certainly the most refined. The human species has learned, during its evolution, that it is not so much *direct* danger that triggers the attachment system as the *statistical degree* of danger. It is not the concrete danger (the predator) that triggers the attachment system, but rather those situations in which a predator may *possibly* appear, in which hunger and thirst may be *possible*, and in which an individual may *possibly* get lost.

The situations that are related to danger are sharply defined in ethology: being alone; too many unknown factors; darkness; open spaces; heights (one can then be easily recognized as prey); fast-approaching objects; and loud, strange noises. When these situations arise, we move into a state of high alert and seek out a safe haven. Bowlby compares the working of these stimuli to that of a traffic light. A traffic light was designed to prevent traffic accidents but is no danger in itself: You can drive through a red light, and the traffic light will not do anything about it. But you know you can count your days if you decide to ignore all traffic lights in the future, and to drive through red. Evolution has programmed us to be afraid of signals that are *connected* to danger, but which, of themselves, are no danger to us. Human beings explore – they seek the more or less unknown, but stop doing this and back off in their attachment system (look for relative safety again) as soon, as it were, as they see an orange or red traffic light. The two most important "red lights" for our attachment system in an organizational context are *being alone* and *too many unknown factors*.

- *Being alone.* It is not hard to appreciate that situations in which one of our ancestors was alone were fraught with danger. Not every situation had the same degree of danger; some, in fact, were completely innocuous, but statistically the best approach was "better safe than sorry." It was better to return to the group ten times too often than once too few.
- *Too many unknown factors.* Situations that contain too many strange elements, too many unknown factors, are also a trigger for our attachment system. Although, as we have seen, we actually have to approach the unknown and our exploration system has us do just that, it is also statistically possible that the situation will contain danger. Thus, when the degree of "unfamiliarity" exceeds a certain level, the attachment system once again resumes control. We cannot state where that level lies, since it varies from person to person. The underlying procedure, however, is identical.

These two factors – being alone and too many unknown factors – are connected to each other. It is unlikely that somebody alone would explore many unknown territories. Conversely, people who feel connected to each other will be able to endure much more of the unknown. In other words, the instinctive triggers reinforce each other – for better or worse.

SURVIVING IN MODERN ORGANIZATIONS

Our present world does not resemble in the slightest that of our prehistoric ancestors, where the evolutionary adaptation process took place for the human species. But we can use these prehistoric times to place human behavior in a broader and more understandable context. The knowledge that darkness, open spaces, and heights trigger the attachment system is of little interest to organizations. The triggers *being alone* and *too many unknown factors* are very relevant indeed. Both seem on the surface to be abstract terms. They may apply to the long-gone prehistoric past or to a child at a garden party. But how are these terms applicable in organizations? How do the *being alone* and *too many unknown factors* triggers actually work in an organization? To understand this fully, we first have to see how the signals that trigger the attachment system change during our psychological development. As children, we accept these signals at face value, but as we grow older, these signals assume an increasingly figurative, abstract, and more complex character. The literal "visibility" of those to whom a child is attached gradually changes to an "availability" of the person to whom that child feels attached at a later age. Initially, the child has to "see" the mother; as it grows up, it is enough for the child to know that the mother is in the house and that she is available if her child needs her. Later still, the availability changes into an internalized *feeling* of support from the attachment figure (for example, the mother or the father), even if they are not physically present at the place where the child – who has by now reached adulthood – requires this availability. In addition, there are personal differences. As the child grows up, so the literal availability of the trusted person is increasingly internalized, and, as such, this becomes the basis for the existential feeling of self-confidence. People who know that throughout their lives they can always rely on the support of the people to whom they are attached will feel less abandoned in difficult moments than those who earlier in their lives received less support.

In an organizational context, *being alone* has a metaphorical meaning. Although adults – just like children – feel uneasy in a situation that is literally strange and unknown, *unknown* takes on a more abstract, metaphorical meaning: It becomes apparent in the behavior of people who feel unpredictability, who do not or no longer understand the rules in the environment, when they feel they are at the mercy of events beyond their control, or when they receive inconsistent (or insufficient or untimely) information. They then look to others for support or withdraw completely. Their energy is directed at personal survival. If, in the organization, there is an environment ruled by, for example, lack of clarity, unpredictability, contradiction, and faulty information, then this is experienced as an excess of unknown factors. There is no direct danger from inconsistency, but then our attachment system is not designed to react to *danger* – it is designed to go into feedback mode (to activate the attachment system) and to stop exploring as soon as it detects too many unknowns when comparing the actual situation with the situation it considers the norm. The attachment system of employees in an inconsistent organization will remain active until the situation is once again considered safe. Employees in such an organization will mainly be concerned with their own position. They will try to avoid situations in which they can make mistakes and have to take risks; they are not really prepared to accept responsibility for a change project that is, of course, always riddled with the chance of mistakes and failures.

Exploratory and stability-centered people are equally concerned by inconsistency. But exploratory people are more likely to turn their backs on organizations, while stability-centered people will try to retain their positions in organizations. Thus, organizations will lose the very people who can kick-start the necessary changes.

If we place the *too many unknown factors* attachment trigger in an organizational context, then it becomes clear how deeply the potential resistance to change is anchored in our nature. It will also become clear that consistent management is vitally important for organizations, which have to be able to adapt constantly to changing circumstances.

From the perspective of the information-intensive, complex, and unpredictable world in which we live, there is an enormous amount of *inconsistency* around us and around the organizations in which we work. If these inconsistent signals become too numerous, then our attachment system puts on the brakes. We then want to withdraw to the safe base of the people with whom we feel emotionally connected and at ease. There is nothing wrong with that. But if there is an inconsistency *within* an organization – the very place where we should feel at ease – then we choose to solve the inconsistency in our immediate surroundings (the organization) before attacking the inconsistency in the world around us. Then we lose the energy and the motivation to take to the exploration trail and actively to look for chances offered by our clients, suppliers, competitors, technology, and everybody else in our environment. It is as if employees are suddenly reduced to pilots who realize that all their instruments have failed and that they are suddenly robbed of all reliable information required to keep them in the air. Then everything is done to get us back on course and discover our position, and we grasp at any straw before tackling other matters. Survival takes priority over everything else.

In terms of attachment, inconsistency means that people lose the *emotional* instruments that make them feel safe in an organization. This has a negative effect on other things than just the ability to change. The effect is considerably broader. If, because of management inconsistency, employees start concentrating on their own survival, then an organization cannot work efficiently and effectively. In other words, there is a direct connection between inconsistency and underperformance in an organization.

Organizations spend a lot of time and money trying to bind talent to them: Performance bonuses, training, and good secondary employment benefits are just a few examples. Organizations also spend a lot of time and money on making the organization flexible and agile. They look for ways of getting their people to look outside the organization and be flexible, and they encourage people to act internally like individual entrepreneurs. Examples of this are the investments in information systems, self-regulating teams, cultural change programs, and so on. Managers hope that they will thus create the flexible, agile organization that is the basis for long-term success. All these investments lose their strength if an imbalance arises between attachment and exploration. This imbalance is caused, as we have seen, by inconsistency.

Let us look at this in another way: An organization that is consistent harvests the fruits of attachment in the form of involvement, identification, and loyalty, and the fruits of exploration in the form of creative energy that is directed at renewal and discovering new possibilities. One of management's most important tasks is to create such a climate in the organization: a climate in which people feel safe enough to explore. By being consistent, a manager or team of managers creates the climate of safety that is necessary if the employees under their command are to develop exploratory behavior. In this chapter, we have clearly shown that feelings of safety are based on *consistency* – a nice word, but an enormous challenge in any practical situation. As we have said, if a management team is to act consistently, then it must devote considerable time and attention to consistency and to the fundamentals that make consistency possible. Acting consistently demands the necessary maturity from managers; that theme is discussed in Chapter 5. But first, in the following chapter, we take a look at the "beacons" of the attachment system, or rather at the different points of orientation that people use to gauge their security, which organizations, particularly those in the high-tech sector, cannot afford to ignore.

4. *Beacons of Attachment*

IN Chapter 2, we looked at the two instincts that can be particularly important for managing organizations in times of turbulence: attachment and exploration. Attachment and exploration are two motives that are always present. Of these, exploration is the most vulnerable; in principle, it requires safe attachment. The beacons that people use to direct them if they are safely attached are apparently not the same for everybody; many look mainly to people, many others look mainly to concepts or things (here collectively lumped together under the term *matter*). In this chapter, we first look at how these different forms of attachment – *people attachment* and *matter attachment* – emerge. Next, we look at the ways in which they differ from each other. Then we deal with a number of questions that arise concerning matter attachment and people attachment, and then ask ourselves how this knowledge concerning matter attachment and people attachment can help free an organization from the prison of S-catraz.

HOW THE ATTACHMENT FOCUS IS FORMED

In the first part of his trilogy *Attachment and Loss*, John Bowlby writes that attachment to a wide range of animate and inanimate objects is possible. The theory about attachment has largely been directed at attachment to people. This is proper, since everything suggests that children, even before the actual stage of attachment, are programmed to direct themselves at people.

In this chapter, I will move away from the idea that attachment is only directed at people, and broaden the focus to include attachment to things and concepts. Because I have opted for simplicity in this book, I will probably charge like a bull in an ethological china shop. But the need to expand the notion of attachment for practical use in management is so obvious that I will ask you to accept this oversimplification – at least in this book – as a necessary evil.

It is useful to make a distinction between what is *learned* and what is *programmed*. The fact that people *do* attach themselves is programmed.

Similarly, the *manner in which* people attach themselves is programmed. This is, as it were, stored in our genes, and the process follows virtually the same pattern in everybody. On the other hand, the *object* of attachment is *not* completely programmed. Apparently, the attachment object must be discovered every single time, and depends on individual personal circumstances. In other words, our instinct has the freedom to attach to different objects. From an evolutionary perspective, that is logical: Childbirth was always a risky business, and there was always the possibility that the mother might die. The child would then also be lost if it had – in a manner of speaking – immediately attached itself to its biological mother. Evolution, it would appear, has built in a pause before the attachment process actually starts. It would seem that this process starts when the child reaches four to six months (and continues until the age of about six), and that the child then attaches to the person or object that is most consistently present during the attachment stage.[1]

Attachment seems to be initially directed at people and then, naturally, at the parents. But the object that is "most consistently present" during this stage may be something other than the parents. It could be a brother or sister, a grandparent, a pet, or an inanimate object such as a computer or book. There are examples, both in humans and animals, in which attachment has been almost exclusively directed at things, although in practice it appears that people who are strongly attached to things and concepts still establish close links of trust with other people. When I refer to matter attachment here, I am not talking about the most extreme examples, but rather about the situations that many of us will recognize in ourselves or in our immediate surroundings and workplace.

The period between the ages of six months and six years seems to be the most sensitive for forming the "blueprint" of the organization of the attachment system. Of course, we can still learn things at a later age. Take, for example, foreign languages, different types of sport, or how to play a musical instrument – but everybody knows that the learning will never be as deep as that which took place as a child. The same seems true of attachment.

For people who have organized their basic attachment around people, I will use the term *people-attached*; for people who have organized such attachment more around things and less around people, I will use the term *matter-attached*. There appears to be a sliding scale: At one end there are people who are extremely people-attached, and at the other there are people who are extremely matter-attached. The largest group of people finds itself somewhere between the two extremes on this scale; some of these people will lean more towards people attachment, others of them more towards matter attachment. In order to avoid any misunderstanding, it should be stated that most people who are matter-attached are not nonattached to people or emotionally left-handed.

The ethological literature describes cases of extreme matter attachment: In such cases, the child attaches itself to inanimate objects because there is no caring person available to whom the child can attach itself. This is not the sort of matter attachment that we have to deal with in organizations, and we shall, therefore, not discuss them further in this book.[2]

RESEARCH INTO MATTER ATTACHMENT

Although there are sufficient examples of matter attachment in ethology, based on observations and experiments, not much attention has yet been paid to it in the human research world. The basis for this concept is therefore largely found in general ethological ideas about the organization of attachment (attachment to that which is most consistently present), the ideas of Bowlby, and the observations of many managers and professionals who immediately recognize the phenomenon in themselves or others, and instantly know how to deal with it.

Bowlby, the father of ethological research, wrote: "There is no reason to think that attachment to an inanimate object indicates anything bad in a child; on the contrary, there is sufficient evidence available that such an attachment can go hand in hand with satisfying relationships with people… Attachment to an inanimate object into later childhood could occur more often than is generally assumed."[3]

In the course of research into attachment in people, the possibility of people attaching to matter has been pushed into the background. *Matter attachment* is a term that is not frequently encountered, and the phenomenon as such is given little attention. In the literature about attachment, the implication is that attachment is always directed at people. This is apparent in the definitions of attachment, which always indicate that attachment is directed at people.[4]

Similarly, in management literature little attention has been given to attachment patterns. The idea of matter attachment as a full-grown and applicable concept in management literature is new. The distinction between managers and professionals, which can partly be explained through matter attachment and people attachment, is not new at all, however. Daniel Couger and Robert Zawacki investigated, for example, the need for social contacts and self-realization in computer specialists. They observed that this group showed (in comparison with other colleagues) a lower need for social contacts coupled with a greater need for personal growth and challenge.[5] That there is a divide between managers and professionals, and that one can actually talk of a cultural barrier between them, is shown in the title of a book by Joseph Raelin: *The Clash of Cultures: Managers Managing Professionals*.[6]

MATTER ATTACHMENT IN THE CONTEXT OF ORGANIZATIONS

Bowlby directed his research at attachment patterns in children. He says in the quotation above that attachment to "inanimate objects" can continue right up to school age. In my own practice as a consultant, my suspicion that this attachment pattern can have a far more permanent character has been confirmed. About 15 years ago, I became convinced that attachment to matter could exist in addition to attachment to people, and that this matter attachment could very well be at the root of the unique and strong aspects that characterize the true professional.

My area of activity was then strongly influenced by the transition I made in my work at the beginning of the 1980s: My role as a psychiatrist became secondary to my role as an organizational consultant. At the start of that period, I came into contact with a research institute where a substantial number of top professionals had become incapacitated. I was asked both to counsel these top professionals, so that they could reenter the work process, and to investigate the possible causes of their disabilities. What struck me at the time was how these professionals would discuss their projects as if they were totally attached to them, as if they were discussing people. The medical department had already decided that these people were suffering from "burnout." I diagnosed, in addition, a complete depression accompanied by many physical ailments.

Because of the corporate culture in this specific institution, there was no possibility of creating a context that would enable them to return to work on a new project. The usual result was permanent incapacity. In order to prevent this early pension turning into a chronic depression, we specifically looked for new attachment objects. This is, essentially, the same as when a person loses a partner or close friend and, after a time, starts looking around to see whether they could possibly find a new companion. One of the people who had been classed as medically incapacitated – a person, incidentally, who recognized the problem and was the first to suggest the term *matter attachment* to me – found a passion for building radio-controlled helicopters and designing software for helicopter-simulation programs. A year before, he had been declared fully incapacitated for work; now, thanks to this new challenge, he became fit and active once again. He found new recognition in the model-building world and in the world of industry. Every trace of depression had disappeared like snow in the sun, without any further need for psychiatric help or medication.

The concept of matter attachment gave the professionals in this organization an insight into the source of their motivation; the instincts behind their choices; their competencies; and their vulnerability. An increasing number of high-tech companies make use of the concepts of matter attachment and people attachment. They show in practice how valuable it can be to incorporate these concepts into company management.

THE DIFFERENCE BETWEEN MATTER ATTACHMENT AND PEOPLE ATTACHMENT

I loved my parents, and still do. They took care of me and taught me how to walk on my own two legs. I will always miss them if they are no longer here… I can still see all those children at school – Eddie, Joan, Mary… I can even remember most of their names… My worst memories of that period were when my grandmother and grandfather died… I have always had a few good friends, some of them for more than twenty years.

I remember the smell of the classroom and the way the sun reflected on the maps and posters hanging on the wall and how the light on a summer's day would slowly move across the wall… I liked geography, all those stories about foreign countries and strange people… oh yes, and dinosaurs. I read everything I could get my hands on about them… and a group of us boys constructed model houses together… No, I can't remember their names, we all went our own way.

In these sketches, we illustrate the differences between two individuals who, respectively, consider themselves to be people-attached and matter-attached. The first story is from a manager, the second is from an engineer.

The famous American biologist Edward Wilson once told about a vacation that he spent in his youth at Paradise Beach, "a small settlement on the east coast of the Perdido Bay in Florida, not far from Pensacola,"[7] as he himself described the location. The following passage from Wilson's story is a perfect example of matter attachment.

There were domestic problems during the summer in my imagination: My parents split up that year. They found it difficult, but I, as the only child, didn't – at least, not at the time. They put me into the care of a family that, during the summer holidays, would offer a place to one or two children.

For a boy like me, Paradise Beach was a real paradise. Every morning after breakfast, I would leave the small house on the sea front and walk along the beach in search of treasure. I would wade through the warm waves, pleased with anything they washed ashore. Sometimes I just looked for a place from where I would stare out over the sea. I would get home in time for lunch, and then out again and back for supper and then out again. Finally I would have to go to bed where I would relive my adventures before falling asleep.

I forget the names of the people I lived with, what they looked like and how many members there were in the family. Probably they were a married couple, undoubtedly kind and generous people. They have slipped out of my memory and I have no desire whatsoever to know who they were. For me, Paradise Beach retains its magic thanks to the animals. I was seven years old and every animal, large or small, was a miracle that needed to be investigated, considered, and – if possible – caught and investigated again.[8]

A second example of matter attachment: A professional writer told me that from a young age he would be found in a corner with a book. Writing, paper, books – those were the things with which he identified. He had to go to a movie studio where they would be filming one of his scripts. In the morning, he felt uneasy, and on his way to the movie studio, he went into a large bookstore that he knew quite well. He stayed there for several hours, and arrived at the studio far too late. He noticed that he had begun to feel better in the bookstore, and he suddenly realized that a close friend from whom he had learned a lot had, a year earlier, died of a heart attack in the very same studio. He realized that he had first gone to the bookstore because he knew that he would feel calm and safe there, so that he could learn to handle the grief that he had apparently repressed.

The following story can serve as an example of people attachment. During a consultation, I spoke to the CEO of a pharmaceutical multi-national. He was a binding element in the industry and, as such, chaired a number of international commissions, handled negotiations between the industry and governments, and was frequently asked to mediate in conflict situations.

He told me that he had had a strong bond with his father. His father was a highly respected professor in inorganic chemistry (a very technical field), and he decided to study this subject as well. The subject, however, had not really appealed to him. His studies went well and caused no problems, but after he had graduated he felt the need to do something else – something that had more to do with people.

He decided to study medicine. But in his third year, not long after the death of his father, his mother became seriously ill. There was not a single moment of doubt in his mind: He postponed his studies and returned home to take care of his mother. When her illness continued, he took a job, under the pretense of being a penniless medical student, as a doctors' representative for a local pharmaceutical company. To his amazement, this went very well: He enjoyed the work and, at the end of the year, was the most successful representative in the company. He had a "kick" every time he visited a doctor – he enjoyed these relationships and working with people. He was promoted to district manager, and a year later he decided finally to give up his ambition to become a doctor. When his mother eventually died and he was once again free, his career shot upwards.

QUESTIONS ABOUT MATTER ATTACHMENT
AND PEOPLE ATTACHMENT

Any brief discussion about the human mind, such as the one we have given about matter attachment and people attachment, can never do justice to the specific and unique nature of each individual human being. The descriptions given here illustrate the main aspects of each type, the "ideal type" if you like, which can help explain the larger and smaller differences between specific individuals. The majority of people are somewhere in the middle of the sliding scale between extreme matter attachment and extreme people attachment. In order to explain these concepts more clearly and to avoid any possible misunderstandings, there follows a number of possible questions about matter attachment and people attachment.

CAN SOMEBODY WHO IS PEOPLE-ATTACHED
COMMUNICATE BETTER THAN SOMEBODY WHO IS
MATTER-ATTACHED?

It is a mistake to think that people who are matter-attached are unable to interact with other people. Just as somebody who is people-attached can be extremely interested in technical matters, so people who are matter-attached can be extremely interested in other people; they can even make it their work. There are, for example, psychotherapists, trainers in social skills, and salespeople with a high degree of matter attachment. They all work with people, but the psychotherapist sees a person as a system, the salesperson sees the customer as a puzzle that has to be solved, and the trainer in social skills sees their subject as a technique.

The psychotherapist who is matter-attached may find the problem more interesting than the person who has the problem. There is nothing wrong with this. On the contrary, it makes it possible for the psychotherapist to maintain the necessary distance from the patient and not be sucked into the problem with the patient. Many professionals who are matter-attached can communicate excellently with their colleagues, particularly if this is about the content of their work. Often, professionals have friends who are also active in the same field.

People who are people-attached will often want to project their own references onto people who are more matter-attached. They cannot, with all their people attachment, understand exactly how it "feels" to be matter-attached. It is a mistake to think that somebody who is people-attached is automatically a better manager. Managers who are people-attached and think within their own parameters of people attachment do not plumb the emotional depths of the professionals they manage – even if they have the best intentions in the world. Managers who are people-attached can thus estrange themselves from matter-attached colleagues, and make them lose their motivation and feel vulnerable, by giving off implicit signals such as "Yes, of course, but when all is said and done, a concept, a project, a thing, a software program (and so on) is not something that you have difficulty in parting company with. OK, it's painful, it's difficult, but to talk about being 'depressed' – come on, now." Actually, it is painful for a matter-attached person to take leave of something like this. Managers who are people-attached underestimate how deeply emotional matter-attached professionals, and particularly the good ones, are concerning the things they do.

An example of the chasm that can form between managers and professionals is shown by this example of a sales support team. One of the team members headed a small quality-management department. He was well known as somebody who was dedicated, and showed inexhaustible energy in bringing projects of considerable complexity to a happy conclusion, by means of extreme attention to detail and of the necessary stubbornness. Total quality management fitted him to a T. In his communication with others, he generally concentrated on content. He only said anything if he was sure he had prepared things down to the last detail – his conviction lay in the content, not the presentation. He was generally a soloist, but he got along very well with the IT department and with external consultants. He worked together with them on a number of projects. But in the last year he had become extremely demotivated. His energy seemed exhausted, he shut himself away, and his output was no longer of the standard to which people had become accustomed.

The facts came to light during a team-building meeting. His manager had, with a single remark, killed a project on which he had been working for nearly a year. "You agree with me, right?" the manager had asked his employee. "Yes, of course," the man had replied. And rationally he *did* agree. But neither he nor his manager realized how emotionally attached the man had been to the project. A decent farewell, a normal period of mourning, was the least that he deserved. The manager had not realized how radical this brusque decision was for his employee, and neither had the employee. The manager believed that a project was just a project – something you could push to one side before starting on something new. The quality manager had, for personal reasons, become very attached to the project, and he felt uprooted – worse, he became depressed. He didn't realize it and didn't know what was happening to himself; neither did his manager.

Without the concept of matter attachment, the connection between the project – which was roughly pulled away from him – and his depression would probably never have been made. When the link was made, the approach was not difficult. In this situation, it was possible to hold an open discussion about the question – and it helped to talk things through. By talking through this "old" question using the theory of matter attachment, both the manager and the professional obtained a better understanding and insight into the situation. This understanding had an influence on the way they worked together. The professional now understood exactly how important certain aspects of his work were to him. The manager understood that something like emotional attachment to concepts, ideas, or techniques actually existed, something that he previously could not have imagined.

"HAS MATTER ATTACHMENT SOMETHING TO DO WITH MATERIALISM?"

Nothing could be further from the truth. People who are matter-attached do not need to be materially minded. If their interest is directed at something material, then it is generally about that particular object, that professional area, and so on. An example: A businessman who deals in classic cars remembers a moment from his youth, when he was about five years old. An uncle had come to visit, driving a car that even then was a classic. While the family sat inside, the boy sat in the car, and since then classic cars meant everything to him. He invested all his money in them. Even today, within the limits of his business, he can go to great lengths for perfection and shows attention to even the smallest detail. He is now internationally renowned as a restorer and dealer, but is not at all concerned with material possessions with the exception of his cars.

"HOW IS SOMEBODY WHO IS PEOPLE-ATTACHED LIKELY TO REACT IF THEY ARE PUT UNDER PRESSURE?"

Somebody who is *people-attached* runs the risk of becoming emotional under pressure. Such a person will, in stressful situations, try to refind their feeling of security in the presence of other people. There is the risk that people will go too far in this, and will end up in forms of psychological dependence (symbiosis).

"HOW IS SOMEBODY WHO IS MATTER-ATTACHED LIKELY TO REACT IF THEY ARE PUT UNDER PRESSURE?"

The attachment instinct is intended to create a bond with something or somebody, with which or with whom you experience the proper sense of security. Somebody who is more people-attached will, as just explained, take a problem to a friend. Somebody who is *matter-attached* will try in the same way to bring the problem to the thing that gives them the greatest feeling of safety: This could be something with which they are working at the moment, or a hobby. This is a perfectly natural reaction, which can be interpreted by the outside world as "locking oneself away." Now, of course, it is often the case that problems cannot be solved if the people confronted with the problems immerse themselves in work or a hobby. Such a reaction does not lead to the solution of interpersonal problems, or of problems that require interaction with other people if they are to be solved. People who are matter-attached and find themselves in such a situation can be helped by intervention from others in order to resolve the stressful situation. At the same time, they may tend to react suspiciously, protectively, and irritably to attention from others. After all, an attempt is being made to remove them from their safe place. The problems or the feelings of stress can actually increase, if the tendency to seek security in content increases and those involved "isolate themselves" further.

When the people in question or the surroundings (managers, for example) do not recognize this pattern, then a vicious circle can arise. The managers notice that the people involved are working longer hours and are more fanatical than ever about their jobs, and can thus draw the conclusion that they are extremely motivated. This conclusion does not contribute to relieving the stress, but actually aggravates the situation. Recognizing this pattern is the first essential step to breaking the vicious circle.

"IS A MANAGER WHO IS PEOPLE-ATTACHED A BETTER MANAGER THAN ONE WHO IS MATTER-ATTACHED?"

Not necessarily. The effectiveness of a manager (regardless of whether they are people-attached or matter-attached) depends on the degree to which that manager is able and willing to understand the references of the other person and to serve the whole organization. Self-knowledge is also a factor: The manager must know what both their strong and weak points are, what effect their behavior has on others, and whether they have found ways to compensate for their own shortcomings. These sorts of factors have a lot to do with maturity. Maturity is the subject of the next chapter.

ESCAPE FROM S-CATRAZ

Springing from one S-curve to another always goes hand in hand with fear and uncertainty. The more unsafe people feel, the more inclined they are to clamp firmly onto that which they trust the most. Alternatively, the safer people feel themselves to be, the easier they can deal with change; they will also have more energy and be more prepared to help define the changes in the organization. It is in managers' own interests to ensure that their employees feel safely attached. In our culture, people attachment is implicitly the dominant starting point. When managers are not aware of the mechanics of attachment, and attachment manifests itself in a wide range of guises, they run the risk of seeing their change process run into resistance. They can get the feeling that they are putting all their energies into the change process, while those people who are supposed to be working with them are behaving passively or cynically. By understanding the mechanics of the matter-attachment and people-attachment processes, managers will be better able to mobilize the knowledge and energy in people to the benefit of the necessary changes.

Anybody who is matter-attached seeks their safety largely in the content – often technical – of their work. If projects are stopped or departments disappear as a result of a reorganization, then people who are matter-attached can experience this as a personal loss. This means that managers who supervise these changes have to treat these as such. At Hewlett-Packard, for example, a manager organized an evening with his team in order to say farewell to a project they had worked on together, which had been stopped prematurely. This manager understood that he had to treat the project as something to which his people had become attached. Taking leave of people is a way of showing respect both for the departed one and for those who are left behind; the same is true when taking leave of projects or organizational units. By organizing the evening, the Hewlett-Packard manager showed respect for the feelings of his team members, who had put heart and soul into the project. In this way, he created space for a new project. By saying farewell, a new beginning could be made.

People who are matter-attached seem more vulnerable to inconsistency than those who are people-attached. People who are people-attached have a better-developed feeling for relationships between people. By talking to other people, they learn a lot more about what is going on than their matter-attached colleagues, who are more inclined to withdraw and reach their own conclusions. People-attached people receive more information about the context in this way. They can then more easily place remarks made by management within this context, and therefore experience less inconsistency. Because people who are matter-attached have less acute antennae for catching subtle social interactions, they can develop a certain suspicion about the "politics" within the organization. Also, they are more inclined than their people-attached colleagues to take an off-the-cuff remark by one of the managers as some sort of formal declaration. A manager who understands this interaction will give even more attention to clear and frequent communication – and thus create an environment of safety and mutual trust.

In addition to clear and frequent communication, a manager will need to invest in other ways of keeping in touch with matter-attached employees (in comparison with the ways they use to keep in touch with people-attached employees). The manager who does not take the time to understand what the employees are doing thereby blocks the road to real contact with them. Matter-attached people largely make contact with others by discussing the *content* of their work. If they notice that somebody is not interested in that, this not only means that there are very few other ways of maintaining contact, but also that they feel *personally* rejected. A manager who does not understand this interaction, and keeps on trying to establish contact by talking about personal things, will be disappointed. They have the feeling that they are investing in a relationship but getting nothing in return. These mutual misunderstandings are a source of "interference" and make it extremely difficult – if not impossible – to create the environment of safety and consistency that is so essential for escaping from S-catraz.

5. Maturity in Complexity

In the previous chapters we have "explored" attachment and exploration. It is obvious that we should try to bring all this together in a model that describes the diversity in people in terms of exploratory versus stability-centered behavior, and people attachment versus matter attachment. In the following chapter we will attempt to make things more concrete and condense them into a model.

Such a model would, it seems, allow us to define people according to their specific strengths as these relate, for example, to the various stages of the S-curve and the way in which they feel attached to their surroundings.

That results in a matrix with the degree of stability and exploration on one axis, and the degree of matter attachment and people attachment on the other axis (you can look ahead to the next chapter if you want to get a better idea of this here). Such a matrix describes, with all the restrictions that are inherent in any model, a blueprint of personalities. To this I have added an additional dimension, which I call *maturity in complexity*: the degree to which people can translate their experience in life to dealing with an ever-increasing degree of complexity.

DEALING WITH COMPLEXITY

An important human instinct is the need for control of the surroundings. This is an instinctive need, and at school (and in later life, too) we are raised in a Newtonian framework about the sustainability and predictability of our environment. We learn to understand the world as if there were a logical cause and effect to it. This Newtonian philosophy has influenced us more than even Isaac Newton might have wished.

This cause-and-effect concept does not work so well in a world that is getting ever more complex. The complexity philosophy that has arisen since World War II has gradually penetrated management thinking, and gives a much more fundamental answer to how complex environments should be approached.

A simple example: Fifty years ago, weather forecasters would probably have said that they would be able to predict the weather if they had large and powerful computers. Now we realize that even with the most powerful computers, we can only predict the weather for a few days at the most, simply because the weather is a complex, chaotic system that is truly arbitrary, at least in part.

Best sellers from Peter Senge, Margaret Wheatley, and Stephen Covey give management the tools that allow them to understand a little better the logic of the complex systems, and to apply this knowledge to organizations and personal leadership.

Maturity in complexity can be described as "the ability to respect complexity, not to avoid paradoxes, to accept dilemmas, and not to fall back on simplification by seeing every event as part of a cause-and-effect cycle."

It is all about being able to see the bigger picture and to reveal the interdependency between the constituent parts. This capacity depends both on the skills and the degree in which people:

- are open to feedback from the environment
- can postpone their own judgment
- want first to understand others before wanting to be understood themselves
- can see their own contribution as part of a whole
- can help connect people
- have insight into their own strengths and weaknesses
- can listen attentively
- can develop from an "egocentric" thinking to a "we-centric" attitude.

This list is incomplete and can be considerably extended. Stephen Covey (*The Seven Habits of Highly Effective People*) and David Cooperrider (*Appreciative Inquiry*) are examples of thinkers who have developed methods of leadership around the personal ability of people to turn themselves into a contributory part of a system.

Maturity in complexity is not the same as experience: Somebody can have considerable experience yet still make the same mistakes. It is not the same as being talented or professional: Somebody can be extremely talented, very good in a specific profession, but can still fail to make use of that talent or profession because they are unable to connect with the environment. Similarly, maturity in complexity is not the same as adulthood (at least not in terms of age): Somebody can be 65 and still think they are the measure of all things.

Maturity in complexity describes the ability to deal with complexity. It is an extension of "Ashby's law." This law, from one of the founders of cybernetics, Ross Ashby, describes the phenomenon that a certain system can only control its environment to the level of its own complexity. Take as examples a streetcar, a car, and an aircraft. A streetcar [tram] can be driven in one direction: forward or backward. The "cockpit" of a streetcar is very simple. The car can move in two directions – that of the streetcar, plus right and left. The "cockpit" of a car is more complicated than that of a streetcar, but nowhere near as complicated as that of an aircraft, which can move in a third direction – up and down.

The same is true psychologically. Somebody with little maturity in complexity will not be particularly effective as a manager. As people gain experience, so they learn to recognize more accurately the complex patterns of an organization and of interhuman relationships. In an organization, there are a lot of parallel developments, and thus many S-curves can be identified: the development of products and services, the running of departments, personal career development, and so on. The organization, too, has an organic dynamic that can be represented in an S-curve. The ability to recognize, accept, respect, and use these various processes in an organization is an ability that grows as maturity in complexity increases. (The review of this dynamic is shown in Chapter 1, Figure 1.8, point 7.) By recognizing these patterns and combining them with an increasing insight into strengths and weaknesses, the organization can become increasingly effective.

A high maturity in complexity is not only important for managers and leaders. As a specialist becomes more mature, their influence will increase and with it the effect of their contribution. If they are able to see their specialty as part of a larger whole, and when they understand the dynamics of that larger whole and put this knowledge to use, their contribution will be of considerable importance. Maturity in complexity is all about having respect for the complexity of that with which you have to deal: Then you no longer need to deny that complexity (through simplification), nor to make use of complexity as an excuse for doing nothing.

MATURITY IN COMPLEXITY IS CONSTANTLY GROWING

Maturity in complexity grows as you gather experience in life. You recognize what is happening (both inside yourself and in the world around you) by reflecting on your own actions and by being open to feedback from others. Maturity in complexity increases as you complete your own S-curves: by witnessing what effects certain decisions have had, and by seeing the consequences of these decisions and accepting them. It is, as Covey says, a process from "dependency" to "independency," and then on to "inter-dependency."

I give here a practical example, in which I try to translate the development into the four stages under which all competencies in a multinational in the service industry can be classified.

In this practical example, we categorize the four stages in increasing maturity in complexity as follows:

1 learning to learn
2 dealing with your own professional competencies
3 working in a multidisciplinary manner
4 providing an example to others through consistent leadership.

These four stages are applicable to all disciplines in the organization: from marketing to financial control, from service to product development. The following case exemplifies the four stages.

STAGES IN THE PROCESS OF DEVELOPING MATURITY IN COMPLEXITY

Stage 1: Learning to learn

Growth demands self-knowledge. By learning to reflect on your own actions, and by learning to understand the underlying motivation of that behavior, you can find the freedom to choose the most effective way of acting. The more you become aware of your own pattern of behavior, and the better you understand why you react in a certain way in a certain situation, the easier it is to stop the primary reaction and decide whether that reaction is effective at this time and in this situation. It used to be enough to learn a trade; now, in a rapidly changing world, it is becoming increasingly obvious that any such knowledge is soon out of date. For further professional growth, it is particularly important to understand the way you function in your profession. A characteristic of people at the start of their growth in maturity in complexity is that they give spontaneous and primary reactions. The advantage is that they are able to generate new ideas and a lot of energy without being hindered by their thinking being too nuanced. The disadvantage of the drive, enthusiasm, and creativity of such whiz kids is that they will rarely take into account the surroundings in which they work. Everybody has experience with such whiz kids – people who may produce very good ideas but who are so awkward in the way they approach the implementation in social–organizational terms that they fail to achieve the necessary consensus and continue operating as soloists.

Stage 2: Dealing with your own professional competencies

In a career, stages 1 and 2 often run concurrently. Whether you are matter-attached or people-attached, you are at a stage where you specialize, where you develop your professional knowledge. Experience grows, and a specific role in the organization begins to take shape. The growth path leads towards management or professional status. People at stages 1 and 2 of their growth in maturity in complexity are focused on making a mark as a professional; this is accompanied by a great need to "score."

While stages 1 and 2 are largely about the "I," stages 3 and 4 have much more to do with the connection with others, with the "we."

Stage 3: Working in a multidisciplinary manner

At stage 3, "building bridges" starts to play a role: being able to understand other people in their roles, functions, and disciplines, and being increasingly successful in making a connection with them. People at this stage will increasingly ask themselves: What does this team need under these circumstances, and what can I contribute with my particular strengths?

Stage 4: Providing an example to others through consistent leadership

The more you grow in maturity in complexity, the greater your ability to see the connection between things. Two examples will explain this further.

Example 1. People at this stage are able to understand the functioning of the different parts of the organization and to appreciate their relative value. In addition, they are able to understand the complex underlying relationships between the various company components. They know how to identify action and reaction, cause and effect, in a complex and dynamic company. They respect the complexity but know how the forces in an organization also play a role and how to use them.

Example 2. Mature people understand the value of the various people in a team and, at the same time, are able to forge these individual contributions into a whole that works in a concentrated and productive way to achieve a common goal. It is often pleasant for people to work in a team that is led by a mature person; they feel appreciated and find extra energy from the productive cooperation within the team. Mature people understand what form of leadership is appropriate under each given circumstance. They are able to judge whether they are suitable for that task, or whether somebody else could achieve better results.

Mature people are able to translate their values consistently into daily practice. They become examples for the behavior or culture that they desire. In this way, individuals are able to exert considerable influence on the culture of an organization, regardless of their position. In a period when organizations are becoming increasingly complex, and changes are happening in a faster and more unpredictable way, mature people – particularly in leadership positions – can, thanks to their clear core values, become centers of calm on which people can fall back. In other words, the more mature people become, the more consistent they become.

Even when people have reached a high level of maturity in complexity, they will still continue to grow. Even people who have reached a high level of maturity in complexity have not finished their development. The paradox is that people then develop *permanently* and know how to put themselves into perspective.

This practical example demonstrates that, as maturity in complexity increases, so there is a marked increase in integration and consistency.

Here is another practical example. This time it deals with the individual.

As we have said, maturity in complexity grows as people gain life experience, reflect on the way they do things, and are open for feedback from others. Maturity in complexity increases because people complete their own S-curves, observe the effects decisions have, and acknowledge and accept the consequences of these decisions. In counseling sessions that my colleagues and I have held, we are often confronted with managers between the ages of 35 and 40, whose careers have suddenly "stalled." A few simple questions reveal that they have had a large number of jobs in a short period of time and have never been coached. Often, the person concerned has been labeled "high-potential material" even before they reached the age of 30, and has kept that label for ten years or so. Without anybody actually saying anything about it, that label has somehow evaporated – and this only becomes clear when a certain promotion doesn't happen. It is almost as if a promising career is slipping like sand through your fingers. If the person asks for feedback, then the answer is generally that the (by now ex-) high-potential material does not have the necessary level of maturity in complexity and is unable to stand "above the business." The following is an example from my own consultancy (the name is fictitious, as are all other names in this chapter).

John is a highly talented manager. He is 40 and has already held five positions with full responsibility. Each of these positions was as general manager of an organization with between 500 and 1,000 employees. Each time, his appointment lasted no longer than one or two years. Generally, a conflict occurred with a shareholder, the board of management, or the chair of the supervisory board. In such a conflict, the various standpoints became polarized. For outsiders, the conflict never seemed to be irresolvable, but John decided in each case to resign. Each time, he was justifiably disappointed. Each time, he was determined to stay longer in the organization and really make a go of things. What he left for his successors was an organization that had gone for a turnaround and was once again in good shape. His successors could build further; he never had the chance. His ambition was to operate at top-management level and, considering his experience and competencies, this was certainly a possibility.

John came to me when he had become embroiled, once more, in a conflict with the board of management. He told me that he had received an offer from a headhunter for another job. "It's almost as if they can smell it," he said with a certain pride.

"What's the job?" I asked him.

It turned out to be something very similar to his current job. In fact, it was a rather lightweight job, even though it paid better. This time I confronted him with the fact that there seemed to be a pattern, and it wasn't really going to get him anywhere: The positions he had been offered were all on the same level, and this last one was actually a little lower than his current one. I explained to him that such patterns are often connected to unresolved problems in the past. This unresolved conflict rears its head in ever-changing guises. The only way for him to break this pattern was to take a long, hard look at himself. If he didn't do this, then he would be trapped and would never grow further into that higher level of management functions that was his ambition. "You aren't mature enough. You can't reflect on yourself," I told him, rather undiplomatically. And, in the same tone, I continued: "If you don't do this, then further advice is useless and you might just have to be a failure in order to understand things."

Then I showed John a picture of people on a staircase (Figure 5.1, bottom left). I pointed to one of the figures and said, "Look, he's walking upstairs. That's you." Next, I showed him a second drawing (Figure 5.1, middle) and said, "In this drawing, somebody is walking upstairs. And

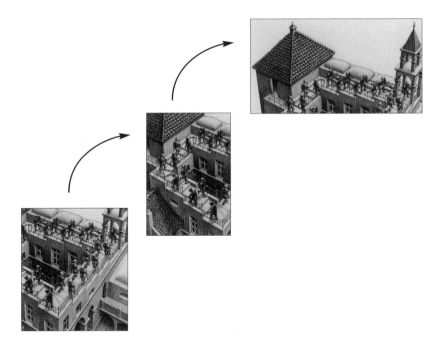

Figure 5.1 *A career moving upwards…?*

that's you." And then I gave him a third drawing (Figure 5.1, top right) – with the same story.

I then said to John, "If you look at each of these drawings individually, then it looks as if you have moved upwards. These three drawings stand for each of the jobs you have done. But if you put the pictures together, then you see it is Escher's staircase (Figure 5.2). And then you see that you haven't been moving upwards at all, but just going around in the same circle. In the first three drawings, it looked as if you were moving upwards, but you forgot to look at the context. If you are mature, you see the context. But you don't do that yet. And remember: The world of board members is very small, and people are going to find out that you always cause problems."

John looked at me as if he wanted to object. But he remained silent and kept looking at the drawings. "What should I do?" he finally asked.

"Offer your apologies to the board of management," I said. "They will accept them. You've been very successful in your job until now."

He hesitated. "Yes, but – "

I interrupted him. "If you don't do this, then I won't do anything else for you."

After a little hesitation, he finally nodded in agreement.

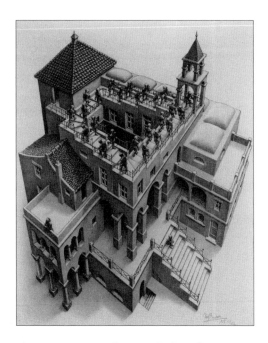

Figure 5.2 But we forget to look at the context
(M.C. Escher, *Ascending and Descending*)

"Next," I said, "take a look at your biography. There has to be a conflict somewhere, possibly with your father or some other figure of authority, and you keep on repeating it. You must accept counseling and at the same time you must look for a coach, perhaps the very chair of the supervisory board that you are now in conflict with. You must talk to your team and take on another role. You have to become the team coach rather than a working foreman. As long as you keep working on the details, they won't grow."

He followed my advice and started working on his biography. His father was a demanding, dominant man who had never really had much time for him and had never paid him a compliment. He projected his anger at this on virtually every figure of authority that he met. Together we looked back on those years and I tried to summarize things: "Each time, you undertook a new assignment as a promising newcomer with charisma and determination. Each time, your part in the assignment ended prematurely because of a conflict. Differences of opinion with boards of management, supervisory chairs, and shareholders are all part of the job. But when a conflict arose, you no longer reacted to the facts but let yourself be carried away by the old anger and reacted like a snotty-nosed teenager of 13 and stuck your tongue out at everybody. As long as you continued doing that, you

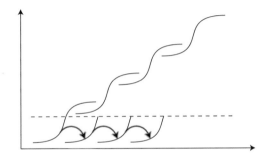

Figure 5.3 The "ceiling" that John needs to get through

remained trapped in a series of short S-curves that all started full of promise and ended with your resignation. You didn't change one little bit. You still haven't completed the most important S-curve: the one of personal growth. Look, I'll draw it for you (Figure 5.3)."

On the left is the road to maturity in complexity – in other words, translating your experience in life into an ability to handle increasing complexity. This is made up of a series of S-curves. The road begins at your birth. You can identify many S-curves in your life. A biography that shows growth is actually made up of critical moments in somebody's life that have resulted in moments that define a new S-curve. That these are often involved with a crisis is natural, because that is the nature of change.

ROUTES TO MATURITY IN COMPLEXITY

Every single person follows their own unique route to maturity in complexity. Every route is a story of a life, just like that of John. This path of growth is different for everybody. No matter how unique each person may be, there are – very generally – a number of differences that can be identified between the routes taken by stability-centered people and exploratory people.

The simplest way of illustrating the growth process of maturity in complexity is the one I drew for John in Figure 5.3: a row of S-curves. Figure 5.4 shows two routes to maturity in complexity: the *explorative route* and the *reactive route*. Exploratory people develop along an explorative route, in which they actively seek out change. Stability-centered people develop their maturity in complexity along the reactive route. They do not consciously seek out change, but react to things they meet in their path. Both routes have advantages and disadvantages.

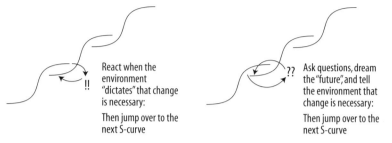

- **Via a reactive route**
  - Do not actively seek out change, but react to changes that present themselves
  - Learn by accepting these changes and embracing them as an opportunity for growth

- **Via an explorative route**
  - Seek out change and create it yourself
  - Destabilize the current situation at the very moment that routine sets in
  - Learn by making mistakes and rejecting stability

React when the environment "dictates" that change is necessary:

Then jump over to the next S-curve

Ask questions, dream the "future", and tell the environment that change is necessary:

Then jump over to the next S-curve

Figure 5.4 *The two routes towards maturity in complexity*

The explorative route

Another example, this time of Susan. Susan had studied at the College for Hotel Management, and then changed directions and accepted a job as manager of 80 IT professionals in a multinational in the high-tech sector. Her answers to my questions are indicative of the way in which exploratory people handle their careers.

I asked Susan, "Why are you making the change?"

Susan: "I felt that in my current job and profession I was in danger of becoming 'stuck.' It was a great job. I learned a lot. Sometimes it was very difficult and I thought about quitting, but now I'm glad I didn't. I like people and enjoy reaching the very best level of service. In the hotel industry, you are constantly confronted with it, often from minute to minute. Quality is an ongoing struggle. I began to love it. Fantastic work. But now, after a few years, I want more. Or rather – something different. As project manager of an international group within our company, I came into contact with e-commerce and the design of a reservations portal. I became fascinated by information technology. The managing of IT professionals seems challenging. I get along well with people, and professionals fascinate me. They can do things that I could never do."

"But," I suggested, "you hardly know anything about the field."

"If I had known it well, I wouldn't have taken the job. I am still relatively young. Things may be different later, but now that isn't an issue. The field has to be new, really new. My colleagues thought I was crazy. I was in line for a promotion and seemed to be heading for a good career. And yet I had this feeling that I had to make this change. I would panic if I imagined that

I was going down a road that I already knew. Then things become routine. That's something I never want. At least, that's how I feel. It isn't rational, but I can't do anything else."

"Isn't there a bit of a risk involved?"

"Yes. Not a big one, but it's there. I could fail. Then my career could be damaged. I could be dismissed."

"Aren't you scared?"

"Yes, I suppose so."

"Doesn't that stop you?"

"You know – I've never thought about it. No. That doesn't stop me."

Susan takes, in her exploratory way, a step in her development. One characteristic is that people in her immediate surroundings don't understand what she's doing. She also does it before other people tell her that she should do it. It is daunting, frightening even, for Susan, but it is typical that she doesn't let that stop her. She has that "must-do" feeling. Anxiety and risk are both obviously present and identified, but do not change the direction of her decision. The people around her react in astonishment because they are looking at the top of the S-curve, while she is actually taking a step over to a new S-curve. Often, other people consider such a decision "irrational" – the surroundings actually consider it a negative step. But anybody who understands that an instinctive imperative – exploration – is at the root of this behavior can see the underlying rationality of the decision.

There are also clear dangers attached to this exploratory attitude – risks that can be a distraction along the explorative route to maturity in complexity. Exploratory people fall into the trap, much more easily than stability-centered people, of changing jobs too quickly. This can mean that they do not fully complete their S-curves; John was an example of this.

The reactive route

Matthew has an amiable and, at the same time, strong personality. He expresses himself thoughtfully and calmly, and can listen attentively. He often summarizes everything that is said, and checks whether he has understood it fully. He is secretary to the board of management in a large company.

"I never knew exactly what I wanted to be, but the principal at my school thought that law would suit me. I finished my law degree. An acquaintance told me about a position that was vacant. I have a high IQ, the company quickly saw my 'potential,' and I was given a four-year plan in which I would have to do several different jobs. Things didn't go well in the second job. Managing people was not my strong point. I didn't realize that at first. I thought I had everything under control. Now I understand things better. Understanding others has never been and still isn't my strong point. (For the sake of clarity, this is not a general characteristic of stability-centered people. P. R.) In each function, I turned out to be the perfect second-in-command. When the secretary to the board of management fell ill, I was asked to fill in for him. After that, I knew what I wanted to do. I first completed the four-year plan, in which I rotated around a number of different functions. This broad experience seemed perfect for the position of secretary. And that's how I reached my current position. Now nothing gives me greater satisfaction than to mail the results of the week's organizing on Friday afternoon, so that everybody can have their documents before Monday morning. I understand the sensitive points, and I can influence to some degree the agenda. I discuss the agenda with the board chair. I am a buffer, and I keep irrelevant or more opportunistic matters off the agenda. I do not participate in politics; I have no feeling for that. That is actually a pro in this job. The balance between work and private life is in order. That is essential, since I am a member of the church committee."

Matthew follows the reactive route. The solutions are offered to him rather than him seeking them out and finding himself in an unknown and risky situation. The advantage that stability-centered people have over exploratory people is that they tend to remain longer in one position and are therefore able to experience the consequences of their own choices and decisions. The risk for them is that if others do not stimulate them or even force them to make a move, then they will stay in the same place and not make full use of their abilities.

THE ROLE OF THE ORGANIZATION IN THE DEVELOPMENT OF MANAGEMENT POTENTIAL

If the organization is to develop management potential, then it is essential that these different routes be fully understood.

Exploratory potentials often have to be kept carefully and justly in check so that they finish their S-curves and have the chance to learn from their own mistakes and successes. Opportunistic human-resources policy and corporate politics often mean that potentials change their jobs far too frequently. Large companies, in particular, lose potentials by neglecting coaching and the natural dynamics of the S-curve in the personal development of their staff. People in such organizations often only realize after some time that they are not really growing in the various jobs they do; they realize they are simply doing the same thing – even if the packaging is different – and still making the same mistakes. An organization that is really concerned about developing talent will have to spend a lot of time *giving guidance* to talent. This guidance must be combined, for better or worse, with the demands made by other company interests, such as the need for vacancies to be filled quickly.

Stability-centered potentials will need to be stimulated to accept a new position. When an organization pays too little attention to the individual, varying styles of learning and development, it is quite possible that a stability-centered person will remain far too long in one function in which they do not develop to any degree. For the person concerned, and for the organization in which that person works, this is an unnecessary waste.

MATURITY IN COMPLEXITY AND CONSISTENCY

In my earlier description of the development stages of maturity in complexity, I mentioned consistency. Since consistency is so important for the change process in an organization, I will here devote a little more time to the relationship between maturity in complexity and consistency.

Maturity in complexity is the ability to deal with complexity. It is all about the ability to become part of a greater whole without losing one's autonomy. Inexperienced white-water rafters will head straight for the finish. They use all their muscle power to move straight ahead. They trust in their own system, their own willpower, their muscle strength, their condition, and their drive to win. If the current is not too strong, they can get by with this. But as the complexity level rises and the currents increase, in combination with higher speeds and the power of the water, the rafters soon realize that they will *not* be able to control everything going on around them in this way; they will notice that they can no longer impose their will on their surroundings. They have to find another way of dealing with their environment. They will learn to harness the power of the water – something that is simply there – in a different way. They will have to learn when to use their power and when simply to "go with the flow." They will learn to act as part of a greater whole. They learn to use the powers around them instead of trying to bend them to their will. They learn that they cannot always reach their goal in a straight line but sometimes have to make a detour. They remain just as focused on their aim, but change the technique they need to reach that aim.

This imagery is easy to understand in an organizational context: Everybody can think of an example of a driven, overenthusiastic, task-oriented, and deadline-oriented young manager. Fewer, but just as well known, are the examples of modest and thoughtful dyed-in-the-wool managers and leaders who say little, listen a lot, and come into action at the crucial moment – managers and leaders who maintain the peace and know how to reduce complex matters to manageable proportions, who know how to get quickly to the heart of things, who use their values as a compass and sounding board. Loving somebody can mean being nice, but also acting strictly. The rafters can at one moment use their strength and at the next "go with the flow." Leaders or managers who are passionate about respect can, at one moment, help employees and then, at the next moment, tell those same employees that they must find the answer themselves. At one moment, it shows respect to help people; at another moment, it shows respect to allow those people to find out something for themselves. *Consistency* means flexibly expressing core values, flexibly moving with the flow of events – but still holding fast to the final goal. Less mature people also have values. But the more mature people become, the better they are able to see the essential strength of the values, and the better they are able to act in accordance with those values, even in a complex environment.[1]

The more you act in accordance with your values, the less disturbing the chaos around you becomes. Chaos no longer takes hold of you; you sit in the eye of the hurricane. Values are the only tools you have for achieving a long-term and constructive effect. It is all about values such as respect for your environment. After all, disrespect means that you want to force your will on the environment without paying any attention to the nature of that environment. This costs a lot of energy and is ultimately ineffective. Managers and leaders who act with respect will also be open in their communications; this is so essential for creating a climate of trust and safety. Other examples of values are trust and the courage and daring that result from it. This trust, in oneself, in others, and in the good result, is necessary if you are to take the jump to the next S-curve, and inspire other people to jump with you. These values are at the core of all actions of leaders who can steer an organization through a major transformation, from one S-curve to the next.

ESCAPE FROM S-CATRAZ

Mature leadership is one of the most important keys for unlocking the prison of S-catraz. Mature leaders are modest: They are not blinded by arrogance or a thirst for prestige. They keep an eye open for their environment: They recognize the various S-curves in their organization, and in the environment in which their organization operates, and act proactively. They are already making the jump to the next S-curve while most of the people in their organization are still enjoying the success of the current S-curve. Since they act consistently from their values, they create the safety in their organization that is essential if it is to retain its exploratory abilities and also to unleash the strength that is essential for leaping from one S-curve to the next – time and time again.

Mature leadership is a necessary prerequisite, but not sufficient in itself to create a changing organization. Equally important is diversity in the organization. An organization can only be resilient – both able to turn new ideas into profits and to make use of existing knowledge while turning down new paths – if it has a sufficient mix of diversity. Changing organizations exist thanks to a mix of stability-centered and exploratory people; mature people and some less mature; people-attached and matter-attached people. That sounds obvious, but organizations, teams, and departments, because of the sort of services and products they offer, have the tendency to become less diverse. This effect is further strengthened because recruitment and team-building seldom look at this aspect of diversity. What this means in practice is discussed in the following chapter.

6. *Diversity*

DIVERSITY knows many forms: diversity in expertise, in gender, in age, and so on. In this book, we only handle those aspects of diversity that are relevant for the changeability of an organization: for the ability of an organization to react alertly to change and to spring from one S-curve to another. This chapter deals with diversity in stability and exploratory instincts, matter attachment and people attachment, and maturity in complexity. People vary in the degree to which they are matter-attached or people-attached. In the previous chapter, we saw how diversity in maturity in complexity also plays a role. An organization needs a mix of people who are stability-centered and exploratory, matter-attached and people-attached, and mature and less mature. This diversity determines the flexibility of an organization.

In an organization, many different growth processes take place in parallel, and thus there are many S-curves that can be identified: the development of products and services, the way departments are run, personal careers, and so on. The organization as a whole also has a dynamic that can be shown as an S-curve. If an organization that is at the end of its S-curve has too many stability-centered people at the top, then problems can arise: People do not realize – or realize too late – that something must change, and have difficulty giving substance to that change. Conversely, an excess of exploratory people can be damaging in an organization that must bring efficiency to its processes and consolidate new products in order to make them profitable (the upward curve of the S-curve). The closer an organization as a whole gets to the top of an S-curve, the more diversity will diminish. People emerge who have all the characteristics of the top of the S-curve: People who are particularly competent in control and feedback (stability-centered people) obtain the upper hand over those who are competent in exploration and feedforward (exploratory people). In Chapter 1, we discussed the need for a balance between stability-centered forces and exploratory forces (the black and white knights of Escher). The managers of an organization must therefore act *anticyclically* to these tendencies.

Another aspect – in addition to the stage in which an organization finds itself – plays a role: The *nature* of the organization also promotes a monoculture, not so much in the area of stability and exploration (although this does happen), but more in the area of matter attachment and people attachment. Consultancies in IT, law firms, group doctor practices, academies, and technical universities often have a vast number of people who are matter-attached and very few who are people-attached. An organization that consists almost entirely of matter-attached people is frequently nothing more than a handful of sand: Everybody does their job, but without any connection to the work of others – cooperation suffers. In such organizations there may be management-development schemes, but little attention is given to support, to the "match" between the development of an individual and the possibilities offered by the organization. The result is that problems can arise in, for example, retaining employees and exchanging knowledge.

In an organization that employs largely people-attached people (for instance, commercial sales and service operations, or hospitals in terms of their nursing staff), there is usually attention for and interest in each other's well-being and that of the customer. There is the necessary attention to career planning and team spirit. Most people in such an organization can retain customers thanks to the good relationship they build up with them and because they understand the needs of the customer. These organizations run the risk of closing their eyes to the possibilities for organizational improvement offered by procedures and technology.

People-attached and matter-attached organizations also differ in the way they deal with change. In a people-attached organization, there is a danger (for example) that the benefits of technical improvements are underestimated. This can result in it making the wrong choices when jumping from one S-curve to another, or neglecting benefits that can be achieved through efficiency improvements. A strongly matter-attached organization will probably acknowledge the possibilities of technology, but will largely ignore the fact that implementing change in an organization is actually the work of people. Such an organization is likely to approach change instrumentally, say by implementing restructuring or a new information system, and think that it has thus realized change. Such an organization will ignore the feelings of those people that have to make a success of the change, with the result that after the initial implementation (the deadline has been met), the actual changes do not lead to the desired result.

It is the task of the managers of an organization to maintain diversity. In order to do this, they must sometimes act anticyclically: At a time when the attention of the organization is focused on increasing the efficiency of processes, the managers must actively look for exploratory people who can develop the next S-curve.

In addition to anticyclical thinking, it is also necessary to make use of the existing diversity – and this is central to this chapter. Three things are required to make use of diversity between people.

1 The differences must be recognized.
2 They must be appreciated.
3 They must be operationalized.

How can we see whether an organization has sufficient exploratory people? How can we see whether a team is suited to its task in the S-curve – whether that is creating a new product or making sure that a production process runs efficiently? In other words, how do we recognize diversity? And how, once we have catalogued this diversity, can we ensure that it is appreciated? And how, consequently, can we put this diversity into operation? These are the matters that we deal with here.

THE AEM-CUBE®: MAKING DIVERSITY MEASURABLE

We have developed an instrument that makes possible the practical application of three core concepts discussed in this book (stability–exploration, attachment, and maturity in complexity). It is called the *AEM-Cube*® and combines the three concepts on three axes (Figure 6.1).

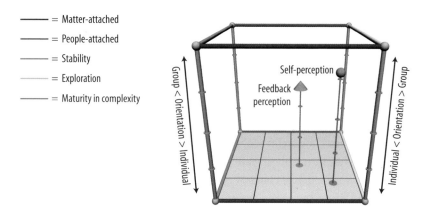

Figure 6.1 *The AEM-Cube*®

92

This instrument has been developed using extensive statistical research. In total, some 700 questions were tested on their relevance and distinguishing abilities. From these original questions, 48 were retained (12 for the attachment axis, 12 for the stability-exploration axis, and 24 for the maturity-in-complexity axis); together they provide a statistically representative result. Next, with the assistance of human guinea pigs, we compiled a database. Using the scores in this database, we are able to compare the person completing the questionnaire with more than 1,000 other people. It is not possible to measure stability, exploration, maturity in complexity, matter attachment, and people attachment using a fixed unit. It is, however, possible to compare scores with each other. The results are thus relative scores, based on percentages. The instrument works best when a person fills out the questionnaire and asks five other people to act as "feedback-givers" by also filling it out. The scores of these five feedback-givers are combined into one average result. In practice, about 70% of the people questioned are given a feedback image that differs substantially from their own self-image. When these differences are discussed, they provide valuable feedback information on the role that the person in question adopts in a team, and the degree to which they use their talents. By placing the results of all team members into a cube there emerges an indication of the diversity, and the strengths and weaknesses, of the team as a whole. None of the positions in the cube have a positive or negative meaning. I shall return to this later in this chapter when I discuss the application of this instrument for both individuals and teams.

Before discussing the cube further, I will first discuss the aspects that it measures.

KEY ASPECTS OF THE AEM-CUBE®: A SUMMARY

Attachment: People-attached versus matter-attached

In order to explore, people have to be able to navigate with the benefit of an emotional beacon of safety. Approximately halfway through their first year of life, people start making a distinction between those people with whom they feel safe and "strangers." The instinct that is at the basis of this is the attachment system. It has evolved over millions of years, in parallel with the above-mentioned exploration system. People can direct themselves at other people but – in the so-called differentiation stage between the second and sixth years – they can also direct themselves at matter (things, techniques, ideas, and so on). In order to be able to manage change in an organization

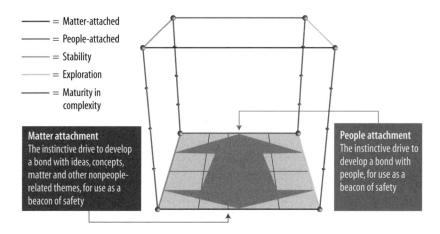

Figure 6.2 *Attachment*

successfully, it is of vital importance to know people's attachment. This all has to do with the feeling of safety and attachment, and – as a direct result – with what people need to handle change easily and/or exhibit exploratory behavior. We can identify a continuum: on the one side people who are extremely people-attached, on the other those who are extremely matter-attached. In the AEM-Cube®, I call this continuum the *attachment axis* (Figure 6.2).

Exploration: Stability-centered versus exploratory

People can deal with information in two basic ways: feedback-directed or feedforward-directed. Stability-centered people are feedback-directed: They concentrate on control, find tangibility important, and contribute to the stability of the organization. People who are feedforward-directed concentrate on an aim in the future. They are less concerned with tangible matters and more eager for change.

Everything that people want to achieve follows the S-curve: It progresses from an intangible idea in the future to a tangible product or service in the present. To make ideas usable, we have to apply an ever-higher level of structure and there is a gradual increase in feedback control. In Chapter 1, I called this "Escher's trap." This dynamic in the S-curve always follows the same course and leads, via success, to an increased rigidity. People possess a deeply rooted exploration instinct, one that has been developed through evolution to look for something new before it is too late – in other words, when that which exists no longer fits in with the changing environment. The quicker the environment changes, the greater the need for exploration. Not all people show the same degree of exploration. We can once again

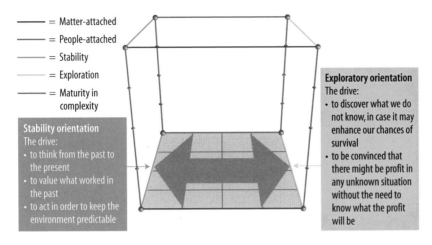

Figure 6.3 *Stability–exploration orientation*

define a continuum: on the one side people who are extremely stability-centered, on the other those who are extremely exploratory. In the AEM-Cube®, I call this continuum the *exploratory axis* (Figure 6.3).

Maturity in complexity

Everybody develops – some to a greater degree, others to a lesser. Everybody is forced to deal in one way or another with the complex world around them. This is the way things have always been, but thanks to the high tempo of change and the impact of modern communications, the complexity has substantially increased. Strict hierarchical structures or organizations that remain unchanged for generation after generation belong to the past. The world has become a network and a living chaos system that organizes itself. Everybody tries their best to "surf" the chaos in order to realize their own dreams, visions, and aims. In order to do this successfully, people have to understand the characteristics of organisms and the workings of self-organization, and be able to make themselves an active component of these. Dealing competently with living organisms (and, therefore, also with organizations) requires life experience: One has to learn to recognize and accept the never-ending cycles of growth, bloom, and decay and the start of new S-curves. The capacity to translate life experience into a competency for dealing with ever-increasing complexity and change is something I call *maturity in complexity*. In the AEM-Cube®, I call this the *maturity-in-complexity axis* (Figure 6.4).

Many people view a low score in maturity in complexity as confrontational. But there is also a growth path that everybody can choose by working

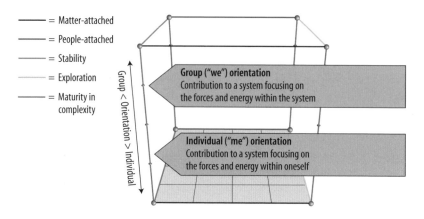

Legend:

──── = Matter-attached
──── = People-attached
──── = Stability
──── = Exploration
──── = Maturity in complexity

Group < Orientation > Individual

Group ("we") orientation
Contribution to a system focusing on the forces and energy within the system

Individual ("me") orientation
Contribution to a system focusing on the forces and energy within oneself

Figure 6.4 *Maturity in complexity*

on self-knowledge and self-management. Apart from the personal path of growth, which one can choose or not, in teams it is truly of complete insignificance whether somebody has a high or low maturity in complexity. Teams without low maturity in complexity (in other words, those teams that score high in maturity in complexity across the board) sacrifice creativity or speed of action. Somebody who is calm and patient often scores higher in maturity in complexity than somebody who is impatient and/or agitated. But it is exactly an impatient person who hammers home their idea, and can act as a creative bull in a china shop, if the team has become complacent. Maturity in complexity scores higher if somebody approaches life realistically (hence, neither too pessimistically nor too optimistically), but sometimes a high degree of optimism can create considerable energy in the person concerned or in the team as a whole. Maturity in complexity is characterized by an effective use of life experience, but many good ideas are proposed by people who are not "hindered by experience" – they are able to generate ideas freely. People who score high in maturity in complexity are generally very capable of binding together extremes in personalities and within the team. The disadvantage is that somebody who is, for example, extremely exploratory can become so involved in the processes that follow from a good idea that the exploratory influence they have in the team diminishes.

THE AEM-CUBE® AS AN INSTRUMENT FOR
REVEALING DIVERSITY

Now we have discussed the three axes individually, we can look at the AEM-Cube® as an instrument. By combining the attachment axis and the

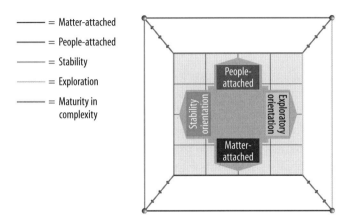

| ———— = Matter-attached |
| ———— = People-attached |
| ———— = Stability |
| ———— = Exploration |
| ———— = Maturity in complexity |

Figure 6.5 *The surface of the AEM-Cube® from above*

exploratory axis, we get a square plane. In this plane, we can identify four basic profiles:

- people-attached and stability-centered
- people-attached and exploratory
- matter-attached and stability-centered
- matter-attached and exploratory.

The third axis, the maturity-in-complexity axis, turns the two-dimensional plane into a cube (Figure 6.5). This axis adds nuance to the four basic profiles by adding a high or low maturity in complexity to each of them.

The way to make the results visible is to compare the results of the individual questionnaire with those of a large norm group. The individual position on the axis is then a relative result, in comparison with others. The units used in these axes are percentile.

WORKING WITH THE AEM-CUBE®: INDIVIDUAL TYPES

Describing individuals as "types" always runs the risk of distorting the truth. A type is nothing more than a means of getting to the truth of the interaction between people, as quickly as possible. A type is no truth in itself, but highlights a number of characteristics that individuals recognize in themselves, and which others see in those individuals. The instrument gains its value in the interaction and the discussion, as well as the thought process, that it initiates. The instrument can reveal what somebody already knows, or provide a surprising new perspective, which, on consideration, can prove valuable and useful.

With these remarks in mind, we can look at the patterns that have emerged thanks to thousands of people who have filled out the questionnaire for themselves in the last few years, and thanks to those who have filled out the questionnaire about other people and have thus provided feedback. The databank that has resulted from this input reveals a pattern of organizational functions. Discussions with each person separately reveal an appropriate pattern of drivers, and of strengths and weaknesses, in the way this person cooperates with others. The following paragraphs give, at a high level of abstraction, the results that have been gathered and assessed during many years of working with the AEM-Cube® in practice. For the sake of space and clarity, I have omitted maturity in complexity in the descriptions that follow. Once again, I would stress that these are simply the main characteristics.

PEOPLE-ATTACHED AND STABILITY-CENTERED

The characteristics of this "type" are as follows (Figure 6.6).

Attention to others
People who score in this quadrant feel at home in a caring role. Important themes are attention, care, and supporting others. People-attached, stability-

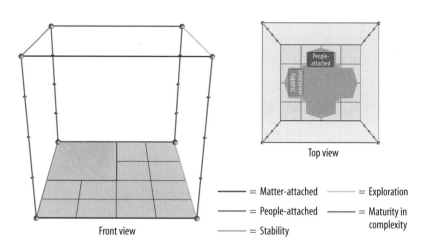

Figure 6.6 *People-attached, stability-centered*

centered people enjoy a good atmosphere and will do their best to maintain it. They are often patient and take time for others. In the stability-centered, people-attached quadrant of the AEM-Cube®, we frequently find people in jobs in which caring for others and taking their needs into consideration are central. Examples are professionals in the health-care sector, relationship management, management support, and people who work in the hotel and catering industry.

Few conflicts
If these people find themselves in a team that is not functioning well, then they generally avoid conflicts. They subordinate their needs to those that they think others may have. In the long run, this results in frustration and repressed pain. The frustration manifests itself – often much to the surprise of others – in a sudden eruption of anger, sickness, or burnout. As people-attached, stability-centered people grow in maturity, they are better able to recognize their own needs, and learn in this way how to resolve conflicts more effectively.

Problems in cooperation
People-attached, stability-centered people have few problems cooperating with other people. They often assume the role of "savior," and field everything that threatens to go wrong. Other people like having them in a team. But they have a tendency to withdraw, and this causes problems for themselves. For these people, one of the challenges posed by growth in maturity in complexity is learning to say no to others, and yes to themselves.

PEOPLE-ATTACHED AND EXPLORATORY

The characteristics of this "type" are as follows (Figure 6.7).

Undertaking something with others
People who score in this quadrant of the AEM-Cube® want to undertake things with other people. Something they could say is: "This looks like a good group of people. I'd like to tackle something with them." Many people in this quadrant are involved in management or consultancy. They have a high sensitivity to the human dynamics of change processes.

Caring for emotional safety
It is a misunderstanding to think that people who are people-attached do not interest themselves in the job or its content. It is, however, a fact that – if a team is not functioning well – they are inclined to ignore the content

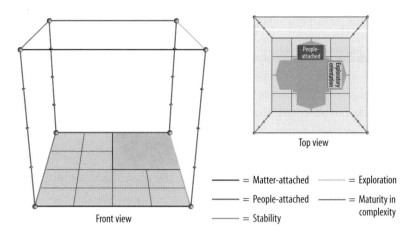

Top view

——— = Matter-attached   ——— = Exploration

——— = People-attached   ——— = Maturity in

——— = Stability   complexity

Front view

Figure 6.7 *People-attached, exploratory*

temporarily, and to invest time and energy in social relations. In this way, they create the situation that is vital for them to be able to work on results.

Directing and leading management

Maturity gives all sorts of people the ability to play an adhesive role between other people. Mature people are, as it were, "bridge-builders," involved leaders of a team or organization. They have the common characteristic that they are emotionally intelligent and can get others to commit to the organization. Effective teams and organizations frequently have such a person with a combination of emotional intelligence and maturity in complexity in a key position.

Dislike of controlling functions

The greatest conflicts and irritations arise with those people who are in the opposite quadrant (matter-attached and stability-centered). It often requires a high level of maturity in complexity on both sides if they are to bridge the gap between them and accept that neither the one nor the other has a monopoly on mutual success.

MATTER-ATTACHED AND STABILITY-CENTERED

The characteristics of this "type" are as follows (Figure 6.8).

Bound by rules and procedures

In this quadrant, we find people who have a controlling or checking role. They feel at home in an inspection or quality-assurance function. While

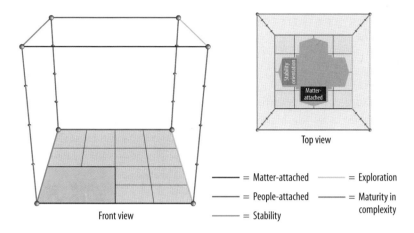

Front view · Top view

——— = Matter-attached   ——— = Exploration
——— = People-attached   ——— = Maturity in
——— = Stability   complexity

Figure 6.8 *Matter-attached, stability-centered*

matter-attached, exploratory people concentrate on concepts, theories, and models, matter-attached, stability-centered people will be more interested in procedures. If a team is not functioning properly, then a matter-attached, stability-centered person is likely to make a proposal aimed at improving the way in which the tasks and responsibilities are allocated. In this quadrant, we frequently find people with an inspecting or controlling role, such as quality control, or in roles where it is crucial to operate within existing boundaries (lawyers, pilots, or accountants).

Problems in cooperation

Matter-attached, stability-centered people can identify strongly with people in the same profession and enjoy maintaining contacts with them. The greatest problems in cooperation arise with strongly exploratory people. A person who is matter-attached and stability-centered tends to raise objections to ideas suggested by an exploratory colleague. Such a person can also tend to point out weak points in a colleague's proposal. This means the exploratory person will often label the matter-attached, stability-centered person as an "eternal chastiser."

The more maturity they obtain, the more matter-attached, stability-centered people learn to use and value their mutual strong points to advantage, and then function as the "supporting beam" of teams and organizations.

MATTER-ATTACHED AND EXPLORATORY

The characteristics of this "type" are as follows (Figure 6.9).

Discovering and inventing

In this quadrant, we frequently find creative professionals in a wide range of areas. This includes the high-tech sector, as well as literature, law, mathematics, archaeology, biology, and so on. People who score in this quadrant are strongly involved in the content of their work. Their need for "innovation" can result in extremely creative inventions, but also in active participation in the content side of changes. People who score in this quadrant frequently have the role of inventor, specialist, creative professional, or project manager.

Creative specialists and team leaders

The accent in this quadrant is primarily on content. The *people-attached,* exploratory person will work with other people because of the *relationship* that person has with other people. A *matter-attached,* exploratory person will work with others because of a mutual interest in the *content.* Such a person is likely to say, "These are people who share my interests and expertise – I'd like to work on something with them." If a team is functioning badly, the matter-attached, exploratory person will likely suggest a brilliant new idea for them to develop together.

Leaders involved with content

Matter-attached, exploratory people can be good leaders. They adopt a different management style from that of people-attached, exploratory leaders.

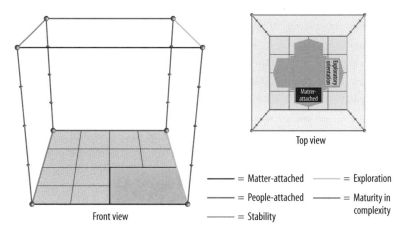

Figure 6.9 *Matter-attached, exploratory*

Matter-attached, exploratory leaders remain strongly involved in the content of the work, especially in the area of their own specialty and allied disciplines. Leaders in this quadrant often receive considerable praise from their specialist colleagues because they understand them and belong to the same area of expertise.

Leaders in this quadrant place far less emphasis on human interaction and all the nuances that this implies. In addition, they are less sensitive to the need of having people-attached people around them. Because of this, they frequently create an environment ruled by content and rationality. This tendency remains even in those with a high level of maturity in complexity. If they actively promote diversity by involving several people-attached people, then they can act as an adhesive element and spur the team on to higher things.

PROBLEMS IN COOPERATION

Matter-attached, exploratory people can often feel hindered by those who are more concerned with procedures (matter-attached, stability-centered people). They consider the contribution made by such colleagues to be extremely disruptive to the creative process, and watch their creative ideas being criticized or even changed to fit in with existing norms. They find this particularly frustrating. They regard such colleagues as superficial and astute (even sometimes Machiavellian), and feel themselves to be out-maneuvered by them.

WORKING WITH THE AEM-CUBE®: TEAM TYPES

Above, we looked at the individual expression of attachment, exploration, and maturity in complexity. The concepts of attachment, exploration, and maturity in complexity also prove valuable in practice to reveal the strengths and weaknesses of a team. In addition, these concepts also make it possible to predict to a certain degree the interpersonal dynamics within a team. The AEM-Cube® can be used for the complete team by combining the individual results and placing them in a cube.

There are various instruments that reveal team roles and diversity in teams – consider those of Belbin and Myers-Briggs. The AEM-Cube® differentiates itself from these instruments on two important points.

- The AEM-Cube® not only reveals diversity and team roles, but also does this for aspects that are of specific importance for changeability.
- The AEM-Cube® places team diversity in a content-strategic framework; there is no such thing as one "ideal" team combination – the ideal team combination depends on the team assignment, the position of the organization, or the department of an organization on the S-curve.

First we discuss how we measure teams ("The average picture"), the role of diversity, and the roles within a team. Next – in the section "Teams in relation to the S-curve" – we include a number of case studies of different types of teams: an exploratory team (at the start of the S-curve), a scale-enlargement team (at the start of the rising line of the S-curve), an operational team (halfway up the rising line of the S-curve), an S-curve extension team (at the end of the S-curve), a team focusing on procedures and costs (at the end of the S-curve), a transformation team (a team that assists in the changeover from the existing S-curve to the next), and an anticyclical team (a team that tracks and initiates the measures necessary for permanent change in the organization).

THE AVERAGE PICTURE

The average picture literally says what it means: an average of the individual scores that have been collected using the instrument of the AEM-Cube®. This average can be shown as one large dot in the cube. This average shows whether a team is largely stability-centered or largely exploratory, and whether the team tends more towards matter attachment or people attachment. The average maturity in complexity shows to what degree the team is able to recognize its own strengths and weaknesses, and to what degree the team is aware that it occupies a place in the larger organization.

Some teams strive for stability, others for exploration. There is a middle area between these two extremes. Later in this chapter, as already mentioned, we will look at examples of the different types of teams.

DIVERSITY

For diversity, we look at how the average is built up. How different are the members of the team when we compare the aspects of attachment, exploration, and maturity in complexity? Are all the members of the team exploratory? Or are they all matter-attached? And do they all score high or low on maturity? If teams have a low diversity, then the team will lose flexibility and become unbalanced: The weaknesses will be magnified and will prevent the strengths being used.

A stability-centered team has the tendency to implode: As the pressure increases, such a team is inclined to become increasingly internally focused, which generally causes the external pressure to increase. Under high pressure, such a team can become paralyzed. Such teams are frequently found in financial or quality departments of large organizations. Departments in governmental ministries can show a similar profile. These teams are good at designing and controlling rules and procedures. As they lack people-attached and/or exploratory colleagues, they run the risk of becoming too internally focused and thus less customer-oriented. They direct their energies inward: They frequently work in their room alone or with other team members. They run the risk of losing sight of the rest of the organization. The more a stability-centered team is matter-attached, the more difficulty the team members will have in developing a team spirit; they will have the tendency to solve problems individually. The learning ability of such a team is low, and so are the effects of synergy within such a team. Often people outside will look on departments such as these as "people in ivory towers who try to conjure up rules without knowing what is actually going on in the real world."

An exploratory team, on the other hand, has the tendency to explode. It bursts with new ideas; the team is only really interested in new things. Once routine threatens to take hold, the team members lose interest and let go. In its relationship with the rest of the organization, the "forward platoon" problem often plays a role: An exploratory team is often so far ahead of the rest of the organization that there is a danger of it becoming cut off.

The key factor for the success of low-diversity teams is the degree of maturity in complexity of the team members: The higher the level of maturity, the sooner they can recognize their own weaknesses and the traps that lie ahead. They will then be more able and willing to take compensatory measures.

THE ROLES WITHIN A TEAM

Diversity by itself is only partly effective. After all, in order to make full use of the potential of a diverse team, the team members must be able to recognize their strengths and weaknesses, and know how to apply themselves for the common good. This demands not only a strongly accepted common goal, but also mutual respect and a certain degree of openness. That is why diversity in a team is not the only important thing; *who* plays *what* role in the team is also important. The contribution that somebody is expected to make must also be appropriate for that person: It is all about the right man or woman in the right place. For example, an exploratory person who is expected to take care of the planning and financial administration of a project can prove damaging to the project and cause a lot of irritation.

The leader's maturity in complexity is of vital importance to the team. A leader with a low maturity level will place considerable demands on the team in terms of maturity in complexity and diversity. What's more, they will be unable to fulfill an adhesive role in the team. They will be inclined to base their actions on the mood of the moment or on their own professional knowledge. They will have more difficulty in creating honesty and mutual respect in their team. Without openness and honesty, the potential of the team's diversity will remain unexploited. A team led by a people-attached leader with low maturity will often suffer from unrest and aimlessness: The common aim will not be adhered to sufficiently, and this will allow events in the organization that often reach the team without being filtered to have a very disruptive effect. A team led by a matter-attached leader with low maturity may often feel that they are not supported in their personal development, and may feel that little attention is paid to their ideas and opinions. The team's common goal is either a matter that is given little attention or is simply more or less enforced. There is too little contact through the leader with the rest of the organization, so that the team is either given too little information or has to make do with information picked up through the grapevine. In all cases, a team led by a leader with low maturity will not easily approach the goal with collective strength and, thus, will not make use of the competencies that are available to it.

A leader with high maturity will be more likely to compensate for a low maturity-in-complexity level in the other team members, because they play an adhesive role. If such a leader is supported by another team member with an equally high maturity level, and who differs from the leader in terms of attachment and exploration, then the team will have a firm basis for achieving an exceptional level of performance. In that case, the lower maturity level of the rest of the team is no problem. On the contrary, as I mentioned earlier, a team that *only* has members with a high level of maturity often suffers from a lack of creativity and dynamics. The less mature members make sure that there is sufficient "life" in the team by suggesting new ideas, and by giving an unexpected perspective, even if this lacks in nuance. During a team-building meeting about the AEM-Cube®, one manager

106

remarked, "I need a few young upstarts to bring some life to things. We shouldn't all be so sensible…"

The contradictions are often highlighted even further in a team with a lot of low-maturity members. A high level of maturity in complexity can build bridges, but also makes people less "sharp." For example, exploratory people, with a high level of maturity in complexity can also sacrifice a little of their exploratory drive. Stability-centered people, on the other hand, sacrifice a little of their conservative attitude as they become more mature in complexity. Matter-attached people come to understand better the interdependency of people, and become more people-directed. People-attached people learn about alternative frameworks of reference, and show more understanding for different perspectives.

TEAMS IN RELATION TO THE S-CURVE

Can we talk about one "ideal" compilation for a team, which is applicable in all circumstances? The answer is no. If we think back to Chapter 1 in which we discussed the S-curve, then it is understandable that both people and teams work better at one position on the S-curve than at others. The talents of stability-centered people are better suited to the middle of the S-curve. The same is true of teams. A stability-centered team has a solid, stable power. It is good at retaining everything good from the past, and is unlikely to throw the baby out with the bathwater. This team is best in the rising middle area of the S-curve, where efficiency plays an important role.

An exploratory team is the opposite. It is revitalizing, hectic, and exploratory. Problems don't exist; for such a team, there are only solutions

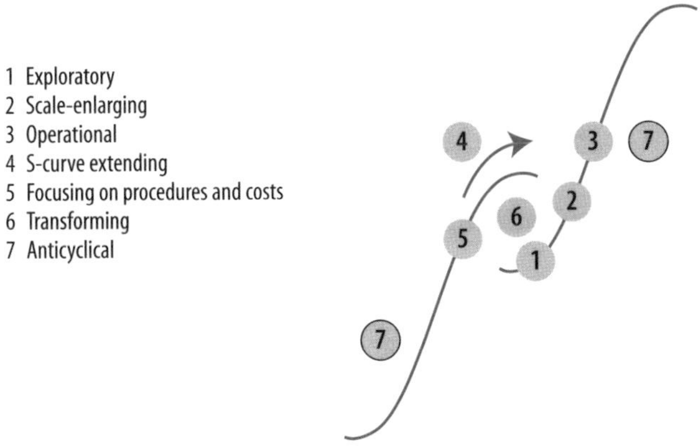

1 Exploratory
2 Scale-enlarging
3 Operational
4 S-curve extending
5 Focusing on procedures and costs
6 Transforming
7 Anticyclical

Figure 6.10 *Team competencies in relation to the S-curve*

and opportunities. This team comes into its own when something really new has to be thought up. In Figure 6.10, the various types of team are shown in relation to the S-curve.

Using these seven team types, we will discuss a number of practical examples. The descriptions will show how attachment, exploration, and maturity in complexity influence the team dynamic, and the strengths and weaknesses, when managing the S-curves in the organization. All cases are taken from my own consultancy practice. The names of the people and companies involved are fictitious.

An exploratory team

A large organization decided to set up a small team of both technical and management potentials to develop a creative business plan for a new company. This company would market technologically superior communication solutions. The team had to use the business plan to interest investors in the new company. It was a driven, enthusiastic team that compiled with verve and a degree of impudence a provocative business plan based on a number of ambitious assumptions. When the team presented the business plan to potential investors, they were disappointed that, although the investors became enthusiastic about the plan, it did not stand up to the rather banal test of attainability. When we look at the team profile in the cube in Figure 6.11, it is obvious that this team fell into their own trap. The feedback scores of the team were all on the exploratory side. The team was not, in this area, very diverse; the team was, however, diverse in matter attachment and people attachment.

In addition, the team had a fairly low level of maturity in complexity, and this meant that the members were insufficiently aware of the trap that was laid by their lack of diversity: All the members of the team were

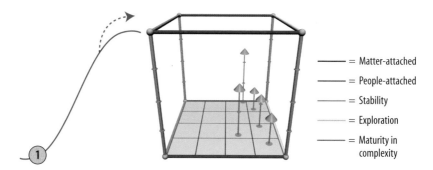

Figure 6.11 *An exploratory team*

exploratory. All team members enjoyed the ideas that the team generated, but did not realize that the team contained insufficient people able to judge the feasibility of the plan. They were only confronted with this lack when they presented their plan to future investors. Once they had gained insight into the compilation of the team, they readily allowed themselves to be assisted by a more stability-centered controller.

A scale-enlargement team

The cube in Figure 6.12 is that of a team responsible for sales in a high-tech industry worth billions of euros. It was responsible for ensuring that new products that had been installed for one or two years with "early adopters" were introduced large-scale into the sales portfolio as a standard product. This team selected the experimental models that were suitable for standardization. The launch of a new standard product involved hundreds of employees and the use of very expensive advertising campaigns. It was vital that nothing went wrong at this stage of the product launch. When making its choice, the team therefore had to take into consideration the commercial feasibility and complexity, as well as the possibilities and limitations of aftersales. This meant that the team – with the necessary tact and care – had to make decisions; launch products on time and within budget; and tell enthusiastic innovators within the company whether their product had made it or not. This team proved particularly suitable for the task. The high level of maturity in complexity of the team members meant that they had a good overview of the dynamics of the organization and the market, understood the demands and expectations of customers and of the creative talent in the organization, and appreciated the demands placed on large-scale sales of these products. In addition, the high level of maturity in complexity allowed them to make full use of their own competencies: The team

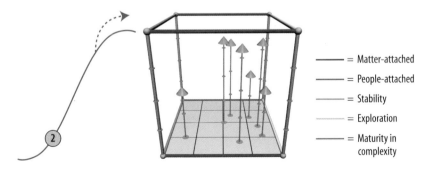

———— = Matter-attached
———— = People-attached
———— = Stability
———— = Exploration
———— = Maturity in complexity

Figure 6.12 *A scale-enlargement team*

is exploratory enough to launch new products, but also has sufficient stability-centeredness to pay attention to the feasibility of the project. The balance between people-attached and matter-attached people meant that the team knew how to handle both the technical and the more emotional aspects of their job.

An operational team

The cube in Figure 6.13 is that of a management team of an organization in advertising, which was extremely successful for several years. The team's core competency was its ability to match in virtually no time the communication needs of a client in specific market segments with specific media. This business is dominated by short-term thinking. Assignments come in several weeks or days in advance, and have to be carried out under enormous pressure. The team members are so attuned to each other that outsiders look on them as a magical combination. The team's horizon is generally no further away than a few weeks. This was, for a long time, no problem. The fact that the team had little diversity – all members were operationally minded, with scores in the middle of the cube – passed unnoticed. The success meant that outsiders did not question the performance or resilience of the team. The low diversity within the team meant that there was no "natural" correction mechanism: The members understood each other perfectly and the cooperation was exceptional. This changed when it became obvious that new developments were arriving in the field of e-commerce. The supervisory board warned on several occasions that choices had to be made concerning an expansion in the services offered – a strategy needed to be developed. Everybody agreed with this in principle, but nobody took the time to determine a mutual position. Meetings that had been arranged to discuss the matter were cancelled or postponed, simply

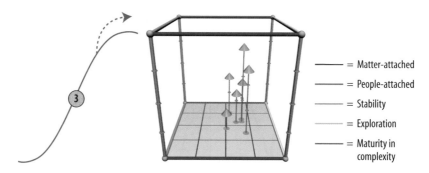

———— = Matter-attached
———— = People-attached
———— = Stability
———— = Exploration
———— = Maturity in complexity

Figure 6.13 *An operational team*

because an urgent assignment cropped up. The remarks of the supervisory board were heard, but no action was taken. The supervisory board did not push the matter; after all, everything was going so well. Here, success worked like a sleeping pill, just as we described in Chapter 1. Gradually it became apparent that investments would have to be made in order to keep up. At the time of writing, various scenarios are being considered. One of the alternatives is to change the compilation of the team so that more diversity results, particularly in the exploratory area. This will allow the team to look further than the problems of now and take the leap to the next S-curve. Another alternative is to allow the company to be taken over by another company. The leap to the next S-curve can then be undertaken in the context of the new company.

An S-curve extension team

The cube in Figure 6.14 is that of a human-resource management (HRM) team of an international company, which has recently grown large, thanks to a number of acquisitions. It had become clear, even before the acquisitions, that both the policy and the systems of personnel administration, management development, and salary administration were rather out of date. The manager of the team suspected that he would have to look explicitly at cooperation within this team if he was to be able to realize the major changes that were ahead. He therefore organized a meeting lasting several days, in which the competencies of and cooperation within the team were explicitly discussed. The team cube was introduced during this meeting. A discussion began – using the cube as a starting-point – about the team's core competencies. Next, a connection was made between these competencies and the issues of the near future: the updating of the systems, whether in relation to the integration of the employees of the acquired

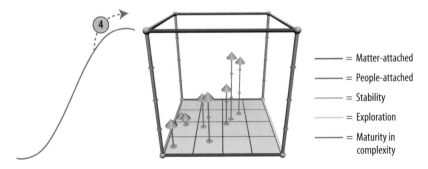

——— = Matter-attached
——— = People-attached
——— = Stability
——— = Exploration
——— = Maturity in complexity

Figure 6.14 *An S-curve extension team*

companies or not. An alternative was to maintain the current systems and to include the new employees in the present out-of-date systems. The team concluded that a conservative approach was the one that had the best chance in the current circumstances: A choice was made to integrate the new employees into the current system. At the same time, the team would be strengthened with a more exploratory, people-attached project manager, who could help the team to keep the change process (the introduction of the new systems) on track.

A team focusing on procedures and costs

The cube in Figure 6.15 is that of a financial team in a medium-sized organization. The feedback scores of the team members show that there is little diversity: All the team members score on the stability-centered side of the cube and all – with one exception – are on the matter-attached side. The team also lacks diversity in maturity in complexity. The team is good at keeping costs under control and making sure that procedures are followed. That is the strength of the team members. It was only during the introduction of an enterprise resource planning (ERP) system that people were confronted with the lack of diversity in the team. The ERP system drastically changed the way of working: A part of the administration system was moved to the line. It became essential that the financial department communicated with the line department to make it clear what their contribution to the financial process was. In the "old" situation, the accent was on retrospective repair by the administrative people in the financial department; in the new ERP system, the aim was to input all information in a single action "at source." The team was inclined – with its accent on stability and matter attachment – to think internally. The low diversity in the team was a handicap in the change process: None of the team members felt at ease in

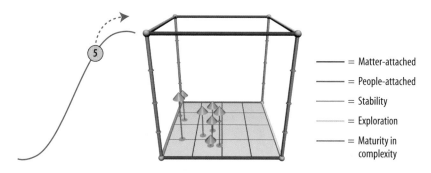

Figure 6.15 *A team focusing on procedures and costs*

a major change process. Discussing the team cube revealed the underlying feelings of unease, and this allowed action to be taken: For the period of the process implementation, the team decided to call in external consultants to help. In addition, measures were immediately put in place to enlarge the diversity within the team, so that in future it would be better equipped to face the changing demands.

A transformation team

The cube in Figure 6.16 is that of a management team of a European travel agency. Thanks to mergers and acquisitions, the travel agency had grown into a company that employed some 100 people. To remain a trendsetter, the agency had decided to design a system that would allow clients to buy their trips on the Internet. This resulted in a large number of reorganizations: Not only the processes had to be changed, but also the organizational structure – the many local offices had to be reduced to a few call centers. During a strategic team session, it became clear that the team had overlooked a number of things. Looking at the mission of the travel agency and at the market developments, it became clear that the highest priority would have to lie in redesigning the process and more or less completely overhauling the IT infrastructure. When the management then looked at its daily activities, it was apparent that its agenda was dominated by questions involved employee satisfaction, management development, and maintaining contacts with the works council. When we look

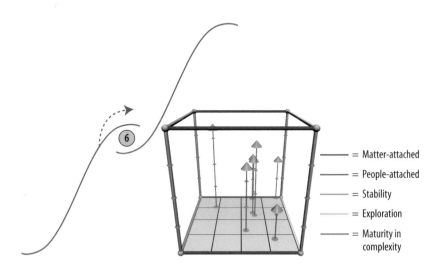

Figure 6.16 *A transformation team*

at the team cube, we can see that this pitfall – much attention to people and less to technical aspects – was predictable. The team consists of people-attached and matter-attached people, but the accent is clearly on people attachment. The people-attached profile of this team was further reinforced by the profile of the chair, who is strongly people-attached: a very extrovert and energetic personality. The manager responsible for IT and for organizing the process restructuring was also considered by his team members to be strongly people-attached; this made the pitfall even more predictable.

An anticyclical team

The cube in Figure 6.17 shows the feedback scores for the management team of a service provider in the area of developing and managing IT infrastructures. The customers of this organization were not satisfied. They thought that the organization did maintain the existing infrastructure very carefully, but that it lacked vision and was insufficiently proactive. Customers remarked that the organization seldom suggested new services and seemed to lag behind in implementing new developments. The customers also felt that the organization had procedural and organizational problems in solving service disruptions. Assuring quality and safety were the core competencies of this organization. These competencies were almost diametrically opposed to the challenge of implementing new technologies in the infrastructure, and to the needs of the customers for a visionary and proactive partner who could constantly come up with new ideas.

In addition, the organization had a large employee turnover, which meant that valuable knowledge was lost. The employees felt little commitment to the organization, partly because they felt that the organization paid insufficient attention to their own professional development.

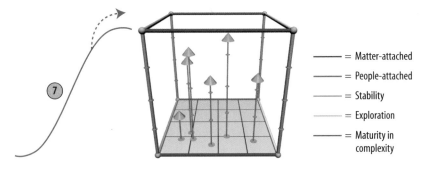

Figure 6.17 *An anticyclical team*

The management team looked at its own competencies as a team in light of these problems. The team showed little diversity in the field of attachment: All the team members scored as matter-attached. The team scored high for maturity in complexity and was – with the exception of two team members – stability-centered. They recognized the need for change, and took this into account in their long-term strategy. They also had a very clear idea of how to put these changes into practice. But they also recognized that none of the team members were naturally talented at giving attention to the employees. They realized that they had too little feeling for motivation, for management development, and for dealing with resistance to change. This was not only made clear by the high staff turnover, but also by the weak innovatory strength of the organization. The managers realized that they approached change in the organization in a predominantly technical manner. The employees in the organization had the impression that their objections to changes were not taken seriously, with the consequence that people left, the changes took longer than planned, and the costs regularly rose out of control. The management team recognized that it had a black hole. They had compensated for this by investing in the human aspects of the change process. They enlisted the help of external consultants in the fields of advice, personal coaching, and support for the change process. The team members became fully familiar with the human aspects of change processes. When the HRM director left, a person who was strongly people-attached and exploratory replaced him. The newcomer introduced greater diversity into the team, so that it was better able to perform an anticyclical role.

VALUING BOTH ENDS OF THE
MATURITY-IN-COMPLEXITY AXIS

In working with the AEM-Cube®, many participants feel as if there is a judgmental aspect to the vertical axis. They say, "The vertical axis has a high and a low end, and it seems that the high end is better than the low end." People might feel negative about scoring low on the maturity-in-complexity axis, and inferior to their colleagues who score higher. It is, however, important to understand that the high and low ends of the maturity-in-complexity axis both have their advantages and disadvantages, depending on the context of the team. That is what I attempt to address in this section.

There are two elements that I would like to highlight concerning the seemingly judgmental nature of the maturity-in-complexity axis. The first is the fact that the maturity-in-complexity axis is the only axis that definitively measures growth. We see people changing over time. We see people in more complex roles functioning more effectively when their maturity feedback score is high, and even better when both their self-image and feedback image are in the same position. That is an observation we cannot deny. (By the way, there is nothing wrong in mounting a personal leadership-growth challenge based on the results of the AEM-Cube®.) The other two axes do not generally measure growth or change. We generally say that if you recognize the pattern in the AEM-Cube® as a correct description and if, for the next year or so, you still believe it is useful and fits your personality, you would do well not to invest too much in changing these aspects of your personality. What you can change is your understanding of yourself, so that you use your personality where you can have success with it. That saves time and frustration, and can focus your resources on your contribution to others. But getting more insight into yourself is generally related both to gaining more maturity in complexity and to achieving a smaller difference between your self-image and your feedback image.

The second point to emphasize, or rather reiterate, is that both the high and low ends of the maturity-in-complexity axis have their own advantages and disadvantages. This can best be illustrated by telling two stories about real business cases. In this way, I hope to convey the message that both ends of the maturity-in-complexity axis need to be valued positively in the right context.

We did AEM-Cube® assessments, and the accompanying consulting process with two teams revealed completely opposite profiles with regard to the maturity-in-complexity axis. One team was exceptionally low, the other team exceptionally high. In both cases, we realized that this "extreme" perfectly fitted their situations, although neither could be considered sustainable in the longer term.

I can mention names for one of the two business cases, but not for the other. The first case concerns the team – led by Barbara Braun, who reported to Jeff Clark, Webb McKinney, and Carly Fiorina – with the operational responsibility for the Hewlett-Packard and Compaq merger. The second case concerns a team in the advertising business with enormous creative power. We start with the latter.

This team comprised top professionals, along with their manager, from a specific business unit of a global advertising company. Each of the team members was famous, successful, and basically a star in their own right. The team had the special mission of delivering extremely creative and innovative approaches to marketing for their clients.

If you look at the team's feedback image, it is immediately obvious how low their score was on the maturity-in-complexity axis (Figure 6.18). The only person scoring above average was the general manager.

What were the characteristics of such a team? It was quite obvious that this team was highly individualistic. Most of the team members expressed themselves competitively and focused on self-expression in whatever form. Most of them also excelled at being creative – including the people to the left of the AEM-Cube®. (Creativity is not the same as being exploratory – sometimes people confuse these two concepts.) The members of this team were typically not capable of staying together without a strong external challenge that could bond them. As long as they had this external challenge, they would work together – day and night, weekends, week after week, if need be.

Most interesting to us were the individual discussions we had with each team member. Two examples stood out. In the pair of profiles in Figure 6.19, you see a self-image (the pink ball) and a feedback image (the green cone). There are two salient features regarding both these highly creative, successful, and individualistic team members: Both their self-image and

Figure 6.18 *A team with very low maturity in complexity, on average*

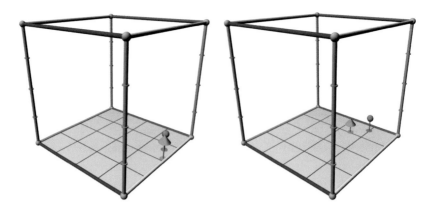

Figure 6.19 *Two managers who decided that, for the time being, they needed to stay low on the maturity-in-complexity axis*

their feedback image scored very low on the maturity-in-complexity axis. It should also be noted that their self-image and feedback image were virtually the same on all axes.

In the discussions and debrief we had with these two professionals, they immediately recognized their profiles. They both recognized their specific characteristics on the two axes that formed the bottom of the cube; as for their scores on the vertical axis, they said that they had decided that, for the foreseeable future, they would *not* be changing their maturity-in-complexity level – not even by so much as an inch upwards. They shared the core belief that in their profession, in their world, low maturity in complexity (combined with the zero difference between self-image and feedback image) was a contributory factor in their success and a key asset for themselves, and quite probably for the team and the organization of which they were a part.

This team was quite well managed by the person with the highest level of maturity in complexity, and its members were able to stay together for as long as the challenge kept them together. Everyone realized the reality of this team: the fact that some key members had categorically decided not to "grow" to maturity in complexity, but to stay individualistic, competitive, and impulsive (with a high level of associated reality-testing). The team members all realized that low maturity in complexity was quite an asset in their profession and industry, and was not something to be thrown away lightly. Understanding this case in its specific context has helped many consultants using the AEM-Cube® to stop thinking negatively about the lower end of the maturity-in-complexity axis.

Now the other case, where the main theme is the complete opposite: a very high level of maturity in complexity.[1] The following case concerns the Merger Integration Office (MIO), operationally responsible for the merger between Hewlett-Packard and Compaq. The group we assessed included a mix of Deloitte consultants and Hewlett-Packard executives.

The most striking feature of this team was the high average level of maturity in complexity that was coupled with the people-attached, exploratory pattern. This pattern is strongly related to high leadership and transformational power. When you see a team pattern like this, you can be sure that this is, and will be, an extremely strong transformational group of people.

We discussed the fact that many participants reported quite a different self-image. Based on individual interviews with all participants, it seemed that some of these people felt that in the politics of the larger corporation (both Deloitte and Hewlett-Packard, although there were more Deloitte people in this group) a high maturity-in-complexity attitude simply wasn't rewarded. They felt that Barbara Braun seemed to have been able to create, within a framework of values, a climate that allowed them to show a higher level of maturity in complexity than they expected to have: They rose to the occasion.

Barbara Braun worked with this team every week, in the time window of its existence, to raise its performance and increase its leadership capacity. She

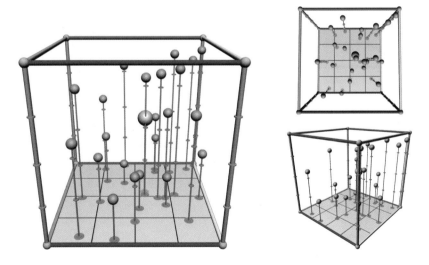

Figure 6.20 *The self-images of the MIO team* (© Human Insight/Hewlett-Packard, 2003)

held high leadership expectations, and found ways to convey these expectations as well as to involve people in most interactions: for many tough-minded executives, probably an inconceivable "waste of time" on the learning side of the balanced business scorecard.

The two team profiles show self-images (Figure 6.20) and feedback images (Figure 6.21). The team averages are shown in Figure 6.22. Figure 6.22 reveals a high level of people attachment and exploratory orientation, together with a very high level of maturity in complexity (close to the 75th percentile).

Such a team, with extraordinary transformational power, was ideally suited to the immense task that they were undertaking. However, this same team would probably lack interest in the operational implementation once the merger required day-to-day direction. This team, at such a high level of maturity in complexity, intuitively understood that change on this scale belonged more to the realm of chaos and complexity theory, and to self-organization: focusing on the practical necessities like connecting IT and financial systems, and downsizing the organization as promised to shareholders. Any more than this was bound to fail, because in such turbulence, with so much anxiety and politics, the organization would not win by focusing on detailed program implementation, and might lose the promise of the merger. It should be added that such realism is part of a very value-driven approach.

However, as soon as the implementation was delegated to the line of businesses, regions, and countries, this team had to be prepared to disband, or to concentrate more on strategy and change and go down a bit in the

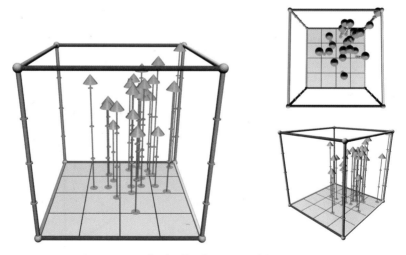

Figure 6.21 *The feedback images of the MIO team*
(© Human Insight/Hewlett-Packard, 2003)

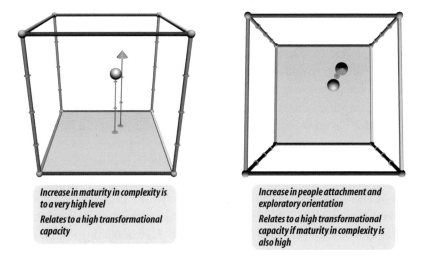

| Increase in maturity in complexity is to a very high level | Increase in people attachment and exploratory orientation |
| Relates to a high transformational capacity | Relates to a high transformational capacity if maturity in complexity is also high |

Figure 6.22 *The MIO team averages of self-images and feedback images*
(© Human Insight/Hewlett-Packard, 2003)

feedforward hierarchy. Otherwise the team might have been perceived as a bunch of philosophers up in the clouds.

The clear message was to *change this winning team* or assign it to a similarly large transformation in the next six months or so, as the S-curve of the merger became more fully developed. This awareness – of perceiving an ideal team for the job in hand, and at the same time understanding that, in relation to the S-curve of the Hewlett-Packard and Compaq merger, this team should be changed – led to the title of this book.

VALUING AND USING DIVERSITY: BUILDING EFFECTIVE TEAMS

There are many ways to give a practical form to valuing (and using) diversity. The most important, as manager, is to create diversity and value it explicitly. This can be done by keeping an eye not only on the content of the work, but also on the process and on the roles people play in a team: Do people listen to each other during a meeting? Can everybody make a contribution? Do people take each other seriously? Can everybody fulfill the role in which they are strongest, regardless of their formal function? A manager who actively does this, and takes corrective action where necessary, creates a well-functioning team.

A way of accelerating this process, or giving a strong first impulse to it, is to organize a team-building workshop. In fact, content and process change places. In day-to-day practice, the content dominates and the process (the *way* in which we work) is shifted to the background; during a team-building workshop, the content forms the framework and the majority of time is dedicated to the process.

An effective team-building workshop can be compared to a burger: The product is "packaged" on two sides. A team-building workshop starts with the following questions: "What do we stand for, and what must be do to achieve our goal? What bottlenecks are we currently experiencing?" At the end of the workshop, the following questions (if things have gone well) generally emerge: "We have learned to know and understand each other better, and have gained some insight into how each of us contributes to the dynamic within the team. What does this mean for the way we handle our assignment? What does this mean for the way we work together in the future? What does this mean for the effectiveness of our team? What does this mean for the way we approach our customers – both external and internal – and our suppliers?"

The result is often that the bottlenecks identified at the start – and even the actual team assignment – are seen in a new light at the end of the team-building workshop. Often, the bottlenecks seem to resolve themselves, or it has become clear that problems "caused by others" are generally largely created by the team itself. During such a process, the team learns how to build a different, more constructive reality.

In order to be able to value and use diversity, it is necessary to obtain an insight into what motivates each team member, how they experience the work, and what blind spots they may have. Approximately 70% of the participants in a team see themselves differently to the way their team colleagues see them. By using an instrument such as the AEM-Cube®, differences are revealed and made manageable. Only by taking time to share these blind spots with each other, and to couple these to everybody's role and competencies, and by working on matters such as trust and conflicts that are taking place in the team, can the team members form a more cohesive team with each other. Blind spots lead to all sorts of misunderstandings – and thus result in inconsistency in communications. Revealing blind spots is more than half the work.

Careful support by an external party is almost always essential. The external consultant makes sure that the process retains its integrity and that participants continue treating each other with respect. Spending two days together like this allows people to practice with the framework requirements that were mentioned earlier when discussing the compilation of a team. Through interaction with each other of this kind, in combination with a growing insight into the team as a whole and the people who together form this team, the trust in the team grows and the underlying commitment to each other is strengthened.

A careful and honest approach is required. Compromises here lead to a failure in team-building. A team-building workshop is *never* intended to judge people. If a manager thinks – based on their own judgment – that somebody does not function well in a team, then they require nothing more than the normal processes of target-setting, coaching, and assessment. If a manager invests in team-building, then it is a sign – come hell or high water – that the team will continue in its present form for the coming year.

One final word: Team-building workshops only have a lasting effect if people stick to the process and give each other fair and open feedback for the months and years ahead.

ESCAPE FROM S-CATRAZ

Attachment, exploration, and maturity in complexity offer tools to map the diversity in organizations and to make the dynamic of a team predictable to a certain degree. In Chapter 2, we discussed how people – and teams – that are highly exploratory play an important role in escaping from the threatening paralysis at the top of the S-curve. We also discussed how stability-centered people are equally important. People can't just keep on inventing; things have to be made tangible. Accurate measurements and a focus on results are just as important as innovation. The cases in this chapter demonstrate clearly that self-knowledge – in individuals and in teams – is just as important as diversity in ensuring that teams play an effective role in organizations.

People are different. And these differences often lead to misunderstandings that disrupt the optimal functioning of a team. But we cannot get by without these differences, because teams made up of people of the same ilk ("only goalkeepers in a soccer team") will not function at their best. If diversity is to be used effectively, then the team members themselves will have to know themselves and each other, and communicate about this; only then can trust be built and maintained.

As organizations develop towards the top of the S-curve, we often see diversity fade away, and people emerge who are largely focused on the characteristics found at the top of that curve. More people appear who have the competencies of feedback and control, and less people are around who have the competencies of innovation and feedforward. If there is one time when leaders should pay particular attention to their human-resources policy, then it is to ensure that an anticyclical diversity – in direct contrast to the characteristics demanded by the S-curve – is maintained.

We have now, in these six chapters, examined the building blocks of change – the ingredients that an organization needs if it is to leap in a quick and agile manner from one S-curve to the next. These building blocks do not, however, form a cohesive story about what a leader must do to develop changeability as a *constant characteristic* of their organization. That is the subject of the next – and at the same time last – chapter of this book.

7. Conditions for a Changeable Organization

THE critical conditions for a changeable organization are *diversity* and *consistency*. Diversity is essential in order to have a "crew" for each appropriate stage on the S-curve; to create effective teams; and to keep an eye on the past, present, and future of the organization. Consistency is necessary in order to create sufficient safety within the organization, so that the organization can take the leap of faith to the next S-curve.

In this chapter, we look at a way of handling a change process that not only achieves the desired *change*, but also increases the company's *ability* to change. We offer recommendations not only for approaching a particular change process, but also for influencing the culture in such a way that the next change processes take place almost automatically.

THE SALMON AS A METAPHOR FOR CHANGEABILITY

In Figure 7.1, we show a salmon springing upstream. We have combined this image with the S-curve – by this time a well-known illustration. The salmon appears to be springing from one S-curve to the next. Before we take a closer look at the challenges posed by change in an organization, we first look at what gives the salmon its ability to "spring" over waterfalls.

A salmon swims upstream in the cold river, urged on by its desire to procreate. The river consists of a number of waterfalls that, like steps on a staircase, bridge a difference in altitude of some 300 meters. Each waterfall is 1, 2, or 3 meters high. The salmon reaches a pool into which a waterfall is cascading; the waterfall is 3 meters high. The water in the pool churns and bubbles. The pool does not allow enough room for the salmon to gain speed for its ascent. Instinctively, the salmon swims into the turbulent water directly under the waterfall. It waits as the water gushes around it. The salmon waits alertly and feels the chaotic forces of the water around it. It senses the current that is pushing towards the surface, right near the waterfall. It swims with full speed into this current and, gathering all its

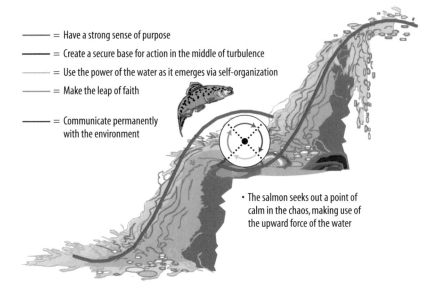

Figure 7.1 *Coping with turbulence…*

strength, it jumps. The salmon continues its journey, mile after mile, waterfall after waterfall, many of them reaching heights of over 4 meters, until it finally reaches its spawning bed. Why can the salmon jump so well against the flow of the river?

1 The salmon is driven by a strong feeling of aim and direction. Its reproductive instincts drive it to the spawning bed.
2 The salmon looks for safety at the center of the turbulence. It uses the center of turbulence to wait for the right moment. Instead of being afraid of chaos and avoiding it, it goes right to the middle of it, and finds the place where the downward and upward currents cancel each other out.
3 The salmon is continuously aware of the turbulent currents in the water around it. It may go to the peaceful eye of the turbulence, but it remains alert and observes everything taking place around it, so that it can make use of the forces present.
4 The salmon uses the forces present in the turbulence of the water. Instead of fighting against the stream, it uses the self-organization of the water, which not only flows downwards but also flows up towards the surface. The salmon uses the force of the water to be able, literally, to fly.
5 Finally, the salmon has the courage to jump: It takes a leap of faith. The salmon cannot hesitate; bears are all too aware of where the salmon

126

hide. The salmon has to swim further to reach its spawning bed. The leap is never without risk, but the salmon has no other choice. It is even more dangerous not to leap.

The metaphor of the salmon shows us the levers that – as long as they are used in parallel and with consistency – make it possible to leap from one S-curve to the next. In the midst of turbulent change, there seems to be nothing other than the current in which we are trapped. The metaphor of the salmon, however, shows us that, even in such situations, there are a number of pointers that we can use to harness the available energy. That energy is always present – even where there is resistance – and can ultimately result in successful change.

The five main characteristics that I have tried to derive from the salmon offer a handy checklist for dealing with complex change: They are the *levers of change* in an organization.

1 Ensure alignment (values, vision, mission, strategy).
2 Ensure consistency (trust and safe attachment).
3 Work on a critical mass (building sufficient support).
4 Focus on value-driven leadership that is well versed in the dynamics of change management.
5 Ensure the best possible communications.

Before discussing each of these levers of change individually, I would first like to look at what it means for an organization to undertake a major change operation.

COMPLEX ORGANIZATIONAL CHANGE
IS A PROCESS NOT A PROJECT

Complex changes demand a different approach than normal project changes. Most of us have been raised in the cause-and-effect school, but we are gradually beginning to realize that complexity demands a different logic. Many of the most important characteristics of organizations, such as integrity, customer-friendliness, quality, concentration on results, cost-consciousness, flexibility, or changeability, are not aims that can be achieved through the simple logic of cause and effect. These characteristics are the result of thousands of daily actions and decisions within an organization. Each of these actions and decisions are so insignificant that the final result cannot be seen as a one-on-one result. It is, for example, impossible to "pour" creativity or innovation into an organization simply by employing a number of creative or innovative people. All sorts of resistance can emerge, which block the path to renewal: The system proves stronger than the individual.

Because things like customer-friendliness, quality, concentration on results, and so on have a much more complex evolution, they can be seen as things that, in complexity theory, are known as *emergent properties*.[1] An example of an emergent property is an anthill. An anthill is a beautifully organized totality, but the organization of an anthill cannot be explained using the logic of cause and effect. All the ants behave according to a number of established behavioral and communication patterns, but there is no logical link that can be made between all these individual behaviors and the shape and compilation of the total anthill. The anthill is strong. If one part of the anthill is destroyed, the anthill repairs itself, just as a wound on the skin heals itself.

Customer-friendliness, changeability, flexibility, and integrity are similarly connected to the behavior of individual employees, just as the form and shape of the whole anthill is connected to the behavior of each individual ant. Core characteristics, such as customer-friendliness, are closely connected in an organization with the culture of that organization. We could jokingly say that culture could be called the "mother of all 'emergent properties' in organizations."

Another way of understanding the concept of emergent properties is given in the following example. Figure 7.2 shows a number of sections of a famous painting by the American artist Edward Hopper (1882–1967). They are shown individually, mixed up together, like unsorted pieces in a jigsaw puzzle.

Figure 7.2 *No emergent property, as yet, in the "jigsaw" pieces*

Figure 7.3 Edward Hopper, *Nighthawks, 1942*
(The Art Institute of Chicago)

Figure 7.3 shows these same pieces, but now put together to show the painting that we all know – *Nighthawks* dating from 1942. The painting evokes in many the feelings of loneliness, coldness, and melancholy. The atmosphere of this painting is an emergent property.

Look carefully at Figure 7.2 with all those separate segments. See whether you can experience these feelings by looking at the first illustration showing the painting in segments, or by looking at just one of those segments. You may be hindered somewhat in this exercise by your knowledge of the painting, but if you try to erase this from your mind, then you will probably discover that the atmosphere of the complete painting is not really present in any one of the segments. If this doesn't work for you – perhaps because Hopper's painting does not conjure up any emotions in you – then try the same thing with something that has made an impression on you.

The message contained in this exercise, and others like it, is that the value of the painting only exists in the *whole* work, and not in any of the individual fragments. What's more, it doesn't even partially exist in any single fragment: If you chop the painting up into ten pieces, that won't result in ten times one-tenth of the emotions; and if you place two pieces together, that won't give you twenty percent of the emotions. It is all or nothing. There is no logical connection between the pieces and the emotions. There is no vague overlapping between the pieces and the whole.

Another characteristic of this sort of complex system is its stability. As soon as an emergent property has achieved a more or less stable form, or shows a recognizable pattern, then it resembles what in the theory of complexity is called an *attractor*[2]: a form that stabilizes itself, that constantly repeats itself, without ever being the same. An anthill is an attractor – it is a complex, well-organized society with a strong regenerating ability that makes it very resistant to problems. If, for example, you cause damage to an anthill by poking around in it with a stick, you will, if you return a little while later, discover that this damage has been completely repaired. An organizational culture has many characteristics of an attractor. A culture does not allow itself to be easily changed: An organization that is internally oriented has the tendency to remain so. An organization that is customer-friendly is customer-friendly through and through. It colors, as it were, everything that takes place in the organization. Because it is a characteristic of the whole organization, this characteristic cannot be easily "destroyed." Newcomers to an organization adapt to this; people who deviate in their behavior will not be employed, will leave, or will be reprimanded for their behavior. Only if there is a large influx of new people who are not customer-friendly, or if a manager is placed in a key position and constantly sends out signals that other qualities are important, can the customer-friendliness be lost. In an organization that has the characteristic of changeability, there is sometimes a degree of inconsistency. But this does not necessarily mean that the next change is more difficult. Only when inconsistency becomes a *pattern* can the "changeability" be eroded.

An organization cannot change itself overnight. To change from one attractor to another requires a lengthy string of impulses, which are all aimed in the same direction. A critical mass must be created that can survive the increasing pressure. If it does survive the pressure, then the organizational system will become increasingly more unstable, until a relatively small incident will push the whole thing from one situation to the next.

The breakthrough – the change from one attractor to another – occurs after a whole range of smaller, yet determining incidents. These large or small incidents are referred to as *defining moments*.[3] These defining moments are visible, crucial incidents – but are not isolated from each other. They derive their power from the fact that they are supported by a whole range of actions, decisions, and choices that all point in the same direction. Defining moments are, as it were, the final push to a new attractor.

Just like all changes, the change from one attractor to another is in fact a leap from one S-curve to the next. When the management of an organization for a long period of time consistently promotes a change, and permanently works on the conditions for the new situation, then a moment occurs when the old organization begins to become unstable. People in the organization reach the point where resistance and pessimism are at their strongest and feelings of anxiety increase in intensity. It is in this period just before the transformation to a new attractor, in the turbulent stage between two S-curves, that everybody in the organization feels: This is it! Increased resistance is normal and is part and parcel of every change process, even those – or perhaps especially those – that are successful.

Daryl Connor describes this as the three stages that each organization goes through: first the stage of uninformed optimism, at the beginning of the change process; then the stage of informed pessimism, as it begins to dawn on people that the process is longer and more complicated than originally thought; and finally, if people persevere, the stage of hopeful realism.[4] Connor points out that it is exactly in the stage of informed pessimism that management must persevere – at the very time that all signals seem to point to the change process being discontinued. Of course it can happen that a projected change process is prematurely discontinued; the sponsors of change allow themselves to be convinced by the intensity of the resistance and end the change process. This stage, however, cannot be avoided, and successful change processes have almost all gone through this stage of informed pessimism.

There is, however, much more taking place in this stage described by Connor. Pessimism is a signal of resistance. But resistance in this stage is more than just pessimism. The resistance emerges from all systems in the organization – both technical and psychological. It is the "struggle" between the old and the new S-curves (Figure 7.4). The change takes place at the top of the old S-curve, where a maximum of feedback systems maintain

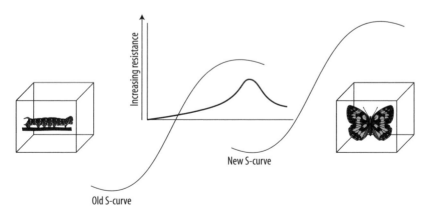

Figure 7.4 *New curves emerge out of a phase of strong resistance*

the stability of the organization. Whether this is an assessment system, a salary system, or an employee that does not want to change, feedback control is everywhere, both inside and outside the human minds. The more these systems are brought out of balance, the more they will try to prolong the old situation. Whether you call it *informed pessimism, resistance,* or *feedback regulation*, it all boils down to the same thing: Every change process, at some point, will seem like a constant uphill struggle. In this period, there is considerable alertness within the organization to see examples that show whether the projected change is being taken seriously or not. If the actions of management are generally placed under a magnifying glass, during this critical stage of change they are placed under a high-powered microscope. The human attachment system tests the consistency of management. People look for proof of consistency so that a safe attachment can be achieved and with it the will to explore, so that everybody in the organization can find the courage to jump to the next S-curve (Figure 7.5).

All this makes three things very clear.

1 We cannot *create* a changeable – or a customer-friendly, or a results-oriented, or an innovative – organization. What we can do is this: Create consistent conditions that allow an organization to develop and preserve such characteristics. Changeability – or whatever other (complex) aim you may have – does not arise through starting a project with milestones, budgets, resources, or time-boxing, but rather through consistently paying attention to the parameters within which the desired results will take place.

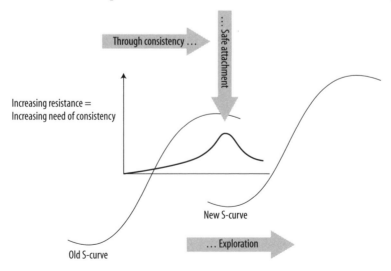

Figure 7.5 *How consistency creates the courage to explore the new curve*

2 In order to achieve the desired change in an organization, it is essential to maintain for a long time a very consistent, alert, and active management of the parameters required, so that the desired result becomes an attractor – a normal situation. Only then is the change truly successful.

3 In every change process, there is a period in which resistance is exceptionally intense. In this stage, the consistency of management is put to the test: There are defining moments that determine the success or failure of the change process. If management reacts to these in line with the proposed change, then it is clear that management is serious about the process. In that case, sufficient trust arises in the organization to allow it to take the leap of faith. If management reacts in a way that is inconsistent with the proposed change, then the people in the organization will lose faith and it will take a lot of time and energy to recreate the momentum for change.

OPERATING THE LEVERS FOR CHANGE
AND CHANGEABILITY

Now that we have taken a look at the character of complex change, we can return to the five levers of change that we distilled from the salmon metaphor.

1 Ensure alignment (values, vision, mission, strategy).
2 Ensure consistency (trust and safe attachment).
3 Work on a critical mass (building sufficient support).
4 Focus on value-driven leadership that is well versed in the dynamics of change management.
5 Ensure the best possible communications.

By applying these five levers together, management can create sufficient consistency to achieve the desired change in a way that makes an organization better for the change, and make a safe environment instead of a dangerous one.

LEVER 1: ENSURE ALIGNMENT
(VALUES, VISION, MISSION, STRATEGY)

Using this first lever, an intangible vision of the future can be transformed into a tangible reality. In this, the whole feedforward hierarchy that we discussed in Chapter 1 is made consistent inside the organization – in other words, vision will match values, the mission will match the vision, and so on.

Values. What values form the foundation of the organization?

Vision. How can this dream be turned into future reality? What role do we want to play in society?

Mission. What components (clients, products/services, technology, images, and so on) can turn this vision into reality? In other words, what is our organization's mission?

Strategy. What are the main things we have to do to achieve our mission? Which road do we choose to take us to our goal?

Tactics. Taking into account the current situation and our short-term expectations, how can we best serve the strategy in the short term?

Process. Taking into account the short-term choices, what must we actually do to achieve these choices? How do we organize ourselves in terms of people, aims, and means?

Structure. What structure will allow us to run the process as well as possible?

Procedures. What procedures can help us run the process with a minimum of costs and a minimum of mistakes? How do we make our performance measurable?

Norms. What information will give us insight into the degree to which we abide by our agreements? How can we gain this insight as early as possible so that we can take corrective action if required?

If we want the feedforward hierarchy to act as a lever for change – and for changeability – then there must be a consensus within the management team about the whole content of this feedforward hierarchy. No step can be ignored: Consensus about strategy without consensus about values and vision has no effect. The day after the strategic conference, unexpected events will occur that will cause each member of the management team to react differently. The strategy has landed, as it were, in quicksand.

In other words, the sequence of the feedforward hierarchy is organic: The charisma, the effect of the values and vision, these are the most important; they "color" the whole organization. Values and vision are emergent properties; they come to life in the behavior of the members of the organization. Thanks to *their* visibility and *their* role, the example set by managers is crucial. It forms the identity of the organization and determines each of the subsequent steps in the feedforward hierarchy.

134

The effect of the norms at the other end of the feedforward hierarchy is the least important. Norms are nothing more than measuring scales or target figures that can be changed without affecting the essential character of the organization.

In practice, it will become apparent that without consensus about values and norms, being *consistent* as we have described here will become an impossible tour de force. People will have the inclination to reach agreements on even the smallest detail, and these agreements will assume the character of an inflexible harness rather than a supple, albeit adhesive, axis along which all activities can develop. Such inflexible agreements not only apply a brake to changeability, they also prove unable to withstand the pressures of daily practice, so that their ability to ensure consistency is negligible. Even worse: The inability to respect such agreements will further feed inconsistency.

We see here an apparent paradox: Organizations that have difficulty in changing see values, vision, and strategy as things that can be easily adapted to new circumstances or fashion. The values and vision are then matters that are so insignificant in the daily practice of an organization that their adaptation is seen as a purely cosmetic paper change that doesn't really matter to anybody. The adaptation of procedures and (performance) norms is often viewed in such organizations as a major intervention. Procedures and norms have become, in rigid organizations, beacons of stability and safety, because the underlying "components" of the feedforward hierarchy (values, vision, mission, strategy) provide insufficient footing.

In a changeable organization, the values and the vision are the most stable elements, and norms are the most flexible. In a changeable organization, the values form the basis for security, and the vision and strategy are (in descending order) the beacons of stability. A changeable organization does not easily change these elements of the feedforward hierarchy, because they are recognized as the core of the organization. The greater the stability an organization has in its values and vision, the greater its changeability. The more stable an organization is in its values, the more flexible it becomes in its aims and structure, in the form in which the values (and the vision and the mission) are expressed.

If the norms do not match the procedures (and the procedures do not fit in with the chosen structure, process, and so on), then in practice there will be too many fractures – too many moments in which actions do not match the agreed goals. People will see this as inconsistency. They will not be able to find the energy, will become confused, and uncertain – and all this will frequently be hidden under a critical, cynical layer or a lack of initiative. On the other hand, if the feedforward hierarchy is "right" and its components are consistent with each other, then this releases an enormous amount of energy in the organization that is put to use in realizing the aims.

For the way in which Carly Fiorina made use of this hierarchy, I would refer you to Chapter 1. For literature that belongs to the very best in management research, I would refer you to the work of Collins and Porras: *Built to Last* and *Good to Great*. There is, in my opinion, no better source of research for showing how essential alignment is between the various components of the feedforward hierarchy.

LEVER 2: ENSURE CONSISTENCY (TRUST AND SAFE ATTACHMENT)

In Chapters 2 and 3, I discussed the relationship between attachment, exploration, and consistency. Most managers understand how essential consistency is in matters of content, but then neglect or underestimate the enormous impact trust (or the lack of it) can have on the functioning of an organization.

If we, as parents, are inconsistent, then we are immediately confronted with the results in the form of inconsistent behavior from our children. In organizations, this causal connection between the behavior of the management and the behavior of the employees is much more indirect in character, and it is often difficult to see it sharply. It is difficult to place the finger exactly on the consequences of either consistency or inconsistency. In addition, it takes time to nurture trust.

In Chapter 6, I presented the AEM-Cube® as a model that can facilitate team-building. From my many years of experience with team-building workshops, it has become increasingly clear to me that if trust is to be developed within a team, then time must be paid to the following seemingly "common-sense" questions.

- Who are the team members? What are their personal motives? What matters are essential to them (personal values)?
- What does each team member plan to contribute to the team objectives, and what expectations do the other team members have of that specific team member?
- What effect does the action of one team member have on the others (practicing giving open and constructive feedback)?

These questions are not only appropriate during a team-building workshop; in daily practice they will also always be in the background. Answering the questions listed above stimulates insight, understanding, and trust in a team. Mutual trust speeds up the decision-making process and increases the reaction time of the team: When team members trust each other, they feel free to approach each other about content in a businesslike and direct manner, and where necessary to enter into conflicts. These conflicts do not harm the relationship, because everybody has taken the time to get to know everybody else. Because of this, each team member feels that their uniqueness is honored, and therefore they can honor the uniqueness of the others. In this way, the diversity within the team can be used to the full.

LEVER 3: WORK ON A CRITICAL MASS (BUILDING SUFFICIENT SUPPORT)

Just like the salmon, which, on its journey upstream, constantly investigates to see whether there are enough forces to work in its favor, so the people in an organization will constantly check to see whether the circumstances are right to jump to a new S-curve.

While the previous two levers both have a rather general "hygienic" effect on an organization, the third lever – working on a critical mass – is specifically aimed at achieving a desired change. As mentioned earlier in this chapter, many of the aims that an organization has in mind are emergent properties. No single project, no single action can achieve the desired situation or characteristic. A whole range of actions and projects together can, however, achieve this – together they get a sort of self-organizing power; together the initiatives are more than the sum of the parts: an emergent property.

It demands enormous investments in time, patience, perseverance, and insight to get sufficient people – a critical mass – in an organization behind a desired change, and to get them to push through change with all its consequences. Time, patience, perseverance, and insight are even more essential because the resistance of the old situation to change increases even as the required critical mass grows.

Dramatic examples of this type of process happened not so long ago in the merger process between Hewlett-Packard and Compaq. Think, for example, of the internal struggle between Walter Hewlett (the son of cofounder Bill Hewlett) and Carly Fiorina: This finally ended in what amounted to an election battle, which Fiorina finally won, albeit by the skin of her teeth. But even after the merger became a fact, both Fiorina and Michael Capellas (ex-CEO of Compaq) were greeted by a skeptical press, and many employees began wondering where the new S-curve was in a time when the only thing that seemed to be happening was cost-cutting operations.

The Merger Integration Office had the seemingly impossible task of bringing the megamerger to a happy end. At the moment of writing this book, it seemed that the integration had been successful, although – in the wake of Fiorina's departure – the original strategy is still being debated. The AEM-Cube® assessment of this team (see Chapter 6), led by Barbara Braun, showed an exceptionally high level of maturity in complexity for each of the team members. That team characteristic was not at odds with the core condition needed to create a critical mass: the leadership to supply the patience, courage, and understanding to make self-organization possible.

LEVER 4: FOCUS ON VALUE-DRIVEN LEADERSHIP THAT IS WELL VERSED IN THE DYNAMICS OF CHANGE MANAGEMENT

During the chaotic period between two S-curves, in which those directly involved make the psychological transition to the new situation, it becomes apparent that, in the stage of informed pessimism, the call for consistency is what it is all about. Behind resistance, pessimism, and cynicism hides fear rather than aggression.

Even the best change approaches cannot avoid a stage of informed pessimism.[5] If management has, until then, been consistent, then the change process will, at a certain moment, take hold.

In practice, this often occurs with one of those *defining moments* that I mentioned earlier – a moment when the leadership of an organization is tested on its core values, the moments that reveal the true nature of management, and thus, in the process, shape the future. The term was introduced by Professor Joseph Badaracco of Harvard Business School. This concept not only makes an important contribution from an ethical point of view, but also acts as a powerful tool that allows management to show its influence during a complex change process. Consciously dealing with the phenomenon of defining moments is, in this case, the core of leadership at times of chaos. It is the "leap of faith" that the salmon makes at the moment that all the forces seem to be working to its advantage. In times of change, all those involved are more alert to signals that strengthen or weaken the feeling of safety. An implicit, but extremely powerful, way of recognizing feelings of fear and hope is to make conscious use of defining moments.

As we have said, the concept of *defining moments* was introduced by Joseph Badaracco. He describes it as a moment in which somebody is confronted with a moral dilemma and is forced to make an almost impossible choice. This choice is not about a simple deliberation between "right" and "wrong." In his book *Defining Moments: When Managers Must Choose between Right and Right*, Badaracco describes the dilemmas of employees and managers who are forced to prioritize their values. One of the examples he gives is that facing an African American who – in order to gain the custom of an African-American client – is invited to attend an important meeting. He finds this offensive: He has fought throughout his life against prejudice, but now he has been invited to attend *because* of the color of his skin. He works 80 hours a week in order to prove himself in the highly competitive environment of his organization. At the same time, a refusal to attend the presentation could do irreparable damage to his future – a future that he is eager to achieve and for which he has already made considerable sacrifices. In the book, Badaracco examines this sort of choice, one that forces the people involved to acknowledge what things really mean to them, that forces them to decide which value has the higher priority, and which has consequences for them, the department, or the company (depending on the position of the person and the impact of the choice made).

The term *defining moments* is more widely applicable than is suggested in Badaracco's book. It is the most powerful lever in times of change. During change processes in organizations, there are a number of such defining moments. They are moments that, for everybody involved, clearly show – through the reaction or decision of the top man or woman to this one incident – that it is an example that clearly rises above the incident itself. They are incidents that clearly show the will and the true values of the leader, and thus determine the future of the change process.

This one reaction can either kill the change process or give it an enormous impulse forward. Here is an example from my own consultancy practice. Three months after his appointment, the CEO of a large manufacturer of technical equipment thought it necessary to revise the way new products were developed. The general manager of one of the business units – a veteran of the company, and very influential – made it clear that he would not be present at the mobilization meeting to which he and his colleagues, plus a number of lower-echelon people reporting to them, had been invited. The CEO insisted he attend, but he arrived late and left for his hotel room before the end of the first day's session. Although the meeting went well, he spent much of the second day criticizing the purpose of the meeting with small groups of colleagues. In the course of this second day, he told the whole meeting exactly what he thought of the whole thing. The CEO once again explained why he thought the proposed changes were essential. The general manager was absent on the third day: He had apparently got on a plane and returned to the office. The CEO telephoned him and tried once more to convince him. When that failed, the CEO decided to remove the general manager from his job and replace him with somebody more progressive. The news about the incident spread through the organization like wildfire – much quicker than any other news about this change process.

It became clear to everybody that the CEO meant business. If the CEO had taken no action, then he would have sent the signal that he *said* the process was important, but that it would probably not boil down to much in practice. The change process would then have been weakened by that one defining moment rather than strengthened – and perhaps weakened to such an extent that the whole process would never even have got off the ground.

Many managers seem unaware that their actions are carefully scrutinized by employees and constantly analyzed. In uncertain times – such as those during a change process – this scrutiny becomes even more acute. Conflicts will arise that are seen by employees as test cases. A leader who, at such moments, does not act consistently with what they have said, undermines their own credibility and thus causes enormous damage to the chance of success for the change process.

But, *how* can a leader cause emergent properties to appear by reacting "correctly" at the really crucial moments? This can only happen if the leader is an example of the whole, a *pars pro toto*. They must show that they are the carrier of the core values that they say they expect from the whole organization, and they have to show this at the very moment when every-body looks at them and wonders, "Can I trust what they say?" This occurs most frequently in the stage described by Connor as the stage of informed pessimism, the stage in which resistance is at its highest, just before the change to the new normal situation, the new attractor. This stage has already been illustrated earlier in this chapter in Figure 7.4: It shows that this is when resistance is at its greatest and when many people in the organization begin to doubt whether the proposed change can ever be achieved. This is the stage when the need for consistency is at its greatest and when critical incidents (examples of consistency) can, if they are put to good use, achieve the power of defining moments.

LEVER 5: ENSURE THE BEST POSSIBLE COMMUNICATIONS

We can be consistent throughout the four levers already mentioned, but if no information is given (or that information is insufficient or tardy), people will lose their understanding of the world around them. With this, the number of unpredictable variables will, in their perception, increase, and so too will their fear. The attachment system will then be triggered and the exploration system will disappear into the background.

We described in Chapter 3 how people do not react to *direct* danger, but rather to the *statistical degree* of danger – a degree that increases as more unknown factors enter the environment. People who find themselves in a situation where they feel they are receiving insufficient information will start looking for that information themselves on the grapevine. They hope by doing this to reduce the number of unpredictable variables and to strengthen their grip on the environment.

Since information is always transmitted from a personal and organizational context, and received in a different personal and organizational context, there is always interference. Just think of the party game where somebody writes down a sentence and then whispers it in the ear of the next person. That person then whispers into the ear of the next, and so on, until the story has been whispered in the ears of everyone taking part. The last person writes down the story they have received, and this is compared to the original story. Often, the story only slightly resembles the original.

Interference is always around, even in those organizations where people are open and communicate with each other in trust. The story above clearly demonstrates that time and distance are permanent polluters of information. If we are to use communication as a lever for consistency, it is not enough to communicate sufficiently and on time; it is also essential to filter out the interference. To do that, attention must be given to making three inter-related channels of communication consistent with each other: direct (face-to-face) communication via the line, formal (written) communication, and informal (spoken) communication (Figure 7.6).

Communication via the line is the primary communication channel. Formal and informal communication support and strengthen the message that is transmitted through line communication. When these three channels are consistent with each other, then the lever becomes extremely powerful. If these three channels are inconsistent with each other, then much of the benefit of the consistency achieved with the first four levers (alignment,

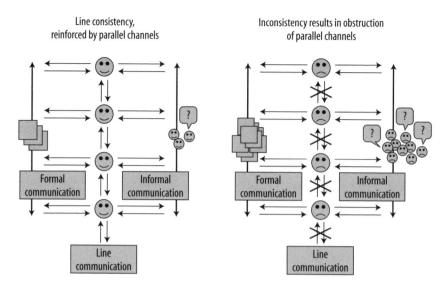

Figure 7.6 *The basic anatomy of internal communication*

consistency/trust, critical mass, focus on value-driven leadership) is destroyed. By either not communicating or communicating inconsistently, the signal of inconsistency only becomes a lot stronger.

In the following section we take a closer look at each of these three aspects.

Communication via the line

When communication must act as a lever for consistency, then it is essential that the primary communication must be via the line, face to face, open, and timely. Communication via the line is important since it gives legitimacy and makes clear that the message is supported by the higher levels of the organization. A staff department communication does not have this power of legitimacy. It is important that communication takes place as much as possible in personal contact (face to face). In personal contact, people get a whole lot of information through their other senses – 80% of their information in nonverbal form. In addition, the feedback loop is short and direct: The dynamics of the interaction, in which telling, reacting, and discussing can take place immediately, ensure that the message is transmitted in its purest possible form. The message can, as it were, start resonating.

Be careful: Openness in communication is not the same as telling *everything*. Telling everything does not necessarily engender trust. People will accept that certain things cannot be communicated. The reasons for *not* telling certain things, however, must be valid and honest.

Just as there is no simple recipe for openness, so there is no simple recipe for timing. Timing is determined by the subject and the context. If people have to read about redundancies in the newspaper, then it is obvious that communication to the employees has taken place far too late. On the other hand, it is neither necessary nor desirable to communicate anything about a possible merger if the intentions of the two parties have not yet been finalized, unless there is a chance that the employees learn of the negotiations from the press.

Formal communication

The second channel is formal communication in the organization, by such written means as memos, newsletters, and employees' magazines. Formal written communication supports and strengthens what has been communicated via the line. If people have been informed by their manager about a proposed change, then when they read about it in a memo, in a newsletter, on the intranet, and through the employees' magazine, this is a strong signal of consistency.

Nevertheless, it frequently happens that formal written communication is used as the primary communication channel. It is tempting to do this. The message can be more carefully formulated and the chance of awkward questions is eliminated. In this way, however, you do not achieve the desired effect, because the receiver does not get important information from another person in the organization. If important information is first communicated in a written form, then the chance is high that the recipient will become suspicious. The more important the information is for the person in question or for the organization as a whole, the less suitable and the less convincing the use of formal written communication as a primary channel will prove. The fact that people are given no opportunity to ask questions or express their feelings only feeds this suspicion: "What is it about this subject that my manager doesn't say a word about it?" Many people will set out to receive confirmation about what has been communicated in a written form. They'll talk to their colleagues and will try, together with others, to interpret the messages. The result is a lot of talk, gossip, and a very active and time-consuming grapevine. Since management from the start avoids direct discussion, this discussion now takes place in the corridors and by the coffee machine (the informal communication channel). At this stage, it is extremely difficult for management to keep the content of the message, as it was originally intended, intact. The message begins to live its own life and take on a whole range of unintended guises. The feelings of insecurity increase.

If formal written communication is to act as a building block for consistency, then it must be a repetition of the story employees have been told by their own managers, or which they have been told in a large meeting where the top management addressed the whole company. In this case, people will see that the original message has been confirmed in writing. As we have already said, this is a very powerful signal of consistency that encourages trust.

Informal communication

The third channel is informal communication. Informal communication is always with us. People constantly check for consistency, to clear away stubborn misunderstandings – even in an organization where trust reigns. In an organization riddled with inconsistency, there is a lot of gossip, people talk about each other, and frequently discuss "conspiracies." In an organization where trust reigns, the informal circuit is much more constructive in tone. Using the informal circuit to strengthen internal consistency demands that you give up the idea of cause and effect: Realize that if you consistently broadcast the same message, sooner or later it will have the desired effect. If management makes an encouraging (or disparaging) remark about somebody in their absence, then you can rest assured it will eventually reach the ears of the person concerned. The more consistent and frequent the messages are, the greater the effect. The informal communication channel, and the amount of gossip and rumors, says a lot about the degree to which management has achieved consistency.

THE FIVE LEVERS: A SUMMARY

In Figure 7.7, we show the approach discussed in this chapter. The timeline (horizontal) shows an increase and decrease in movement, indicating the degree of resistance (vertical). The curve indicates the stages of Connor: uninformed optimism, informed pessimism, and hopeful realism.

Initially, people start a change process with a lot of enthusiasm. They often think that they will simply "get the job done." After a while, it becomes clear that it is not going to be quite so easy: The results do not keep up with the expectations, the old way of doing things seems highly

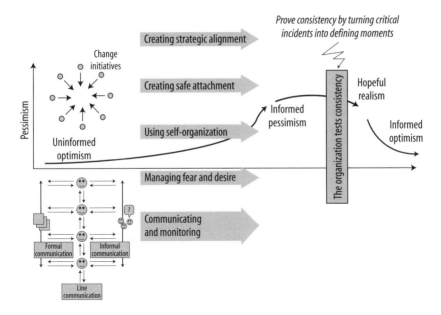

Figure 7.7 *The five levers: A summary*

resilient, the new way has teething problems. Doubts arise in the organization about whether the change process is really necessary and whether it can be achieved. This feeling also creeps over the sponsors. Resistance increases, and this is the time when all eyes are focused on those who initiated and sponsored the change process.

It is at *this* stage of the change process that critical incidents can assume the force of defining moments. These defining moments can herald the success or failure of the change process: They can mean the transformation into a new attractor, but they can also cause the process to fail and leave nasty traces in the organization. These defining moments may seem to be unconnected incidents, but that is an illusion: They are never unconnected. Defining moments derive their power from the fact that they make all the small, often invisible, events, remarks, and incidents much clearer; they allow things to crystallize.

An organization that is aiming for something that has the character of an emergent property will not be able to restrict itself to a single project; this will never bring about the desired change. By using *in parallel* the five levers described in this chapter, you can achieve a complex change in a way that will strengthen the organization's ability to change. As the process develops, an organization will emerge that – at all levels – is capable of reacting adequately and opportunely to changes in the environment.

Notes

Introduction

1 Quoted literally from a speech given at a meeting of Hewlett-Packard shareholders in Cupertino (California) on February 29, 2000
2 In particular, Bowlby, 1969, 1973, 1980; Feeney and Noller, 1996; Lorenz, 1981
3 Talbot, 1998
4 Nicholson, 1998
5 Jones, 1981a, 1981c
6 Bowlby, 1969, 1973, 1980

Chapter 1

1 Collins and Porras, 1994
2 Burrows and Elstrom, 1999
3 Modis, 1998
4 Monod, 1971; Prigogine, 1984
5 Blanchard and Waghorn, 1997; Handy, 1994; Modis, 1998
6 Van der Erve, 1994
7 Shay and Rothaermel, 1999
8 Modis, 1998
9 Katz and Rothfeder, 2000
10 Bernardo Bertolucci in *NRC Handelsblad*, January 16, 2002
11 D'Aveni, 1996
12 Hamel and Prahalad, 1994
13 "Woman in love", sung by Barbra Streisand, written by Barry and Robin Gibb, and published in 1980 by CBS Inc.
14 Pribram, 1976
15 Handy, 1994
16 E-Services World 2000, Paris, March 13, 2000

Chapter 2

1 Monod, 1971
2 Wilson, 1996
3 Bowlby, 1969
4 *Idem*
5 Archer and Birke, 1983
6 *Idem*
7 *Idem*
8 Lorenz, 1981

Chapter 3

1 Kotter, 1999
2 Consistency is an *emergent property*. This term will be explained further in Chapter 7.
3 Peters and Waterman, 1982
4 Collins and Porras, 1994
5 Badaracco, 1989
6 Covey, 1992
7 Badaracco, 1989
8 Badaracco, 1997
9 These blind spots are revealed using tests in which people score themselves on a wide range of facets; other people then score those people on the same facets (360-degree feedback).

Chapter 4

1 Ainsworth, 1978
2 For a description of these forms of attachment, see Bowlby, 1969; Harlow and Harlow, 1972; and Leavitt, 1997
3 Bowlby, 1969
4 Feeney and Noller, 1996; Karen, 1998
5 Couger and Zawacki, 1980
6 Raelin, 1991
7 Wilson, 1996
8 *Idem*

Chapter 5

1 See also Collins, 2001

Chapter 6

1 Thanks to Jim Arena who, on behalf of Barbara Braun, checked and advised us regarding this story.

Chapter 7

1 An *emergent property* is a characteristic that only emerges when the system functions as a whole, irrespective of the components from which it is made up (O'Connor and McDermott, 1997).
2 An *attractor* is a stable situation into which the system will transform (O'Connor and McDermott, 1997).
3 *Defining moments* are actions or events that reveal the current system, test the values and the will of the sponsor of change, and give form to the future (Badaracco, 1997).
4 Connor, 1993
5 *Idem*

Bibliography

Ainsworth, Mary D. *Patterns of Attachment: A Psychological Study of the Strange Solution.* Hillsdale, NJ: Lawrence Erlbaum Associates, 1978.

Ansoff, H. Igor, Edward J. McDonnell, Linda Lindsey, and Stephen Beach. *Implanting Strategic Management* (The Comparative Psychology of Animals and Humans). 2nd ed. Englewood Cliffs, NJ: Prentice-Hall, 1993.

Archer, John, and Lynda I. A. Birke (eds.). *Exploration in Animals and Humans* (The Comparative Psychology of Animals and Humans). Wokingham, Berkshire: Van Nostrand Reinhold (UK), 1983.

Argyris, Chris. *Interpersonal Competence and Organizational Effectiveness.* Homewood, IL: Irwin-Dorsey, 1962.

Argyris, Chris. *Integrating the Individual and the Organization.* New York, NY: John Wiley & Sons, 1964.

Argyris, Chris. *Strategy, Change and Defensive Routines.* Marshfield, MA: Pitman Publishing Inc., 1985.

Argyris, Chris, and D. Argyris. *Moral Reasoning and Moral Action: Some Preliminary Questions.* Cambridge, MA: Harvard University, 1979.

Argyris, Chris, and Donald A. Schön. *Organizational Learning.* Reading, MA: Addison-Wesley, 1978.

Ashby, W. Ross. *Introduction to Cybernetics.* New York, NY: Routledge Kegan & Paul, 1964.

Ashby, W. Ross. *Mechanisms of Intelligence: Ashby's Writings on Cybernetics* (Roger Conant, ed.). Salinas, CA: Intersystems Publications, 1981.

Badaracco, Jr., Joseph L. *Defining Moments: When Managers Must Choose between Right and Right.* Boston, MA: Harvard Business School Press, 1997.

Badaracco, Jr., Joseph L., and Richard R. Ellsworth. *Leadership and the Quest for Integrity.* Boston, MA: Harvard Business School Press, 1989.

Bahlmann, Tineke, and Barbie Meesters. *Denken & Doen, Een studie naar ontwikkeling en strategische heroriëntatie van zes Nederlandse ondernemingen rond een crisis.* Delft: Uitgeverij Eburon, 1988.

Bartholomew, Kim, and Daniel Perlman (eds.). *Attachment Processes in Adulthood.* London: Jessica Kingsley Publishers, 1994.

Bateson, Gregory. *Steps to an Ecology of Mind.* London: Paladin Books, 1973.

Bateson, Gregory. *Mind and Nature.* London: Wildwood House Limited, 1979.

Beer, Stafford. *Decision and Control.* Chichester: John Wiley & Sons, 1966.

Beer, Stafford. *Platform for Change.* Chichester: John Wiley & Sons, 1978.

Beer, Stafford. *The Heart of Enterprise* (The Managerial Cybernetics of Organization). Chichester: John Wiley & Sons, 1979.

Beer, Stafford. *Brain of the Firm.* Chichester: John Wiley & Sons, 1981.

Belasco, James A., and Ralph C. Stayer. *Flight of the Buffalo: Soaring to Excellence, Learning to Let Employees Lead.* New York, NY: Warner Books Inc., 1993.

Blanchard, Ken, and Norman V. Peale. *The Power of Ethical Management.* New York, NY: William Morrow, 1988.

Blanchard, Ken, and Terry Waghorn. *Mission Possible: Becoming a World-Class Organization While There's Still Time.* New York, NY: McGraw-Hill, 1997.

Blurton Jones, Nicholas. "Comparative aspects of mother-child contact." In: *Ethological Studies of Child Behaviour* (ed. Nicholas Blurton Jones), pp. 305–328. Cambridge University Press, 1972.

Bobrow, Daniel G. *Qualitative Reasoning about Physical Systems.* Cambridge, MA: MIT Press, 1985.

Boden, Margaret A. *Purposive Explanation in Psychology.* Cambridge, MA: Harvard University Press, 1972.

Boden, Margaret A. *Artificial Intelligence and Natural Man.* New York, NY: Basic Books, 1977.

Boeke, Kees. *Wij in het heelal, een heelal in ons. Twee tochten door macrocosmos en microcosmos.* Amsterdam/Purmerend: J. Meulenhoff/J. Muusses, 1959.

Bowlby, John. *Attachment and Loss. Vol. 1: Attachment.* New York, NY: Basic Books, 1969.

Bowlby, John. *Attachment and Loss. Vol. 2: Separation (Anxiety and Anger).* New York, NY: Basic Books Inc., 1973.

Bowlby, John. *The Making and Breaking of Affectional Bonds.* London: Tavistock Publications Ltd., 1979.

Bowlby, John. *Attachment and Loss. Vol. 3: Loss (Sadness and Depression).* New York, NY: Basic Books Inc., 1980.

Bowlby, John. *Ethologie, een alternatief voor de psycho-analyse, een kruisingsexperiment.* Nico Tinbergen lezing, Nederlandse vertaling met commentaar: N. Vodegel, interne uitgave Dr. H. v. d. Hoevenkliniek.

Britten, R. J., and E. H. Davidson. "Gene regulation for higher cells: A theory," *Science,* 1969, 165, pp. 349–357.

Burrows, Peter, in Palo Alto, California, with Peter Elstrom in New York, *Business Week Online,* August 2, 1999.

Calvin, William H. *The River That Flows Uphill: A Journey from the Big Bang to the Big Brain.* New York, NY: MacMillan Publishing Company, 1986.

Campbell, Jeremy. *Grammatical Man: Information, Entropy, Language and Life.* New York, NY: Simon & Schuster, 1982.

Campbell, Norman. *What is Science?* New York, NY: Dover, 1953.

Capra, Fritjof. *The Turning Point: Science, Society, and the Rising Culture.* New York, NY: Simon & Schuster, 1982.

Carnap, Rudolf. *Der logische Aufbau der Welt.* Hamburg: Felix Meiner, 1961.

Ceruti, Mauro. *Constraints and Possibilities: The Evolution of Knowledge and Knowledge of Evolution.* Newark, NJ: Gordon and Breach Publishers, 1994.

Chomsky, Noam. *Language and Mind.* New York, NY: Harcourt, 1968.

Churchland, P. Smith. *Neurophilosophy: Toward a Unified Science of the Mind-Brain: Computational Models of Cognition and Perception.* Cambridge, MA: MIT Press, 1986.

Cohen, P. C. *Set Theory and the Continuum Hypothesis.* Menlo Park, CA: W. A. Benjamin, 1966.

Collins James C., and Jerry I. Porras. *Built to Last: Successful Habits of Visionary Companies.* New York, NY: HarperBusiness, 1994.

Collins, Jim. "Level 5 leadership: The triumph of humility and fierce resolve," *Harvard Business Review,* January 2001.

Combs, Allan (ed.). *Cooperation: Beyond the Age of Competition.* Newark, NJ: Gordon and Breach Publishers, 1992.

Connor, Daryl R. *Managing at the Speed of Change: How Resilient Managers Succeed and Prosper Where Others Fail*. New York, NY: Villard Books, 1993.

Cornelis, Arnold. "Filosofie van het nieuwe management als leerproces," *Bedrijfskunde, Tijdschrift voor modern Management*, 1986, 58(2), pp. 133–142.

Cornelis, Arnold. *Logica van het gevoel: stabiliteitslagen in de cultuur als nesteling van de emoties*. Amsterdam-Brussels: Stichting Essence, 1992.

Couger, J. Daniel, and Robert A. Zawacki. *Motivating and Managing Computer Personnel: Business Data Processing*. New York, NY: John Wiley & Sons, 1980.

Covey, Stephen R. *The Seven Habits of Highly Effective People: Powerful Lessons in Personal Change*. London: Simon & Schuster, 1992.

Cypert, Samuel A. *Following the Money: The Inside Story of Accounting's Firm First Mega Merger*. New York, NY: Amacom, 1991.

Darwin, Charles. *On the Origin of Species*. 1859.

D'Aveni, Richard. "Corporate success in an age of hypercompetition." Presentation at the Spring World Congress for Corporate Real Estate Executives, International Development Research Council, Philadelphia, May 6, 1996. Conway Data, 1996. Online at: www.conway.com/philly/philly3.htm

Davis, Martin (ed.). *The Undecidable: Basic Papers on Undecidable Propositions, Unsolvable Problems and Computable Functions*. Hewlett, NY: Raven Press, 1965.

Deal, Terrence E., and Allen A. Kennedy. *Corporate Cultures: The Rites and Rituals of Corporate Life*. Reading, MA: Addison-Wesley Publishing Company, 1982.

Dennett, Daniel Clement. *Consciousness Explained*. Boston, MA: Bay Back Books, 1992.

Dennett, Daniel Clement. *Darwin's Dangerous Idea: Evolution and the Meanings of Life*. New York, NY: Simon & Schuster, 1995.

De Rosnay, J. *Macroscope: A New World Scientific System*. New York, NY: HarperCollins, 1979.

Eccles, John Carew. *The Human Psyche*. Berlin: Springer-Verlag, 1980.

Edelman, Gerald M., and Vernon B. Mountcastle. *The Mindful Brain: Cortical Organization and the Group-Selective Theory of Higher Brain Function*. Cambridge, MA: MIT Press, 1978.

Eldredge, Niles. *Reinventing Darwin: The Great Debate at the High Table of Evolutionary Theory*. New York, NY: John Wiley & Sons, 1995.

Emery, F. E. (ed.). *Systems Thinking*. 2 vols. Harmondsworth, Middlesex: Penguin Books, 1981.

Feeney, Judith A., and Patricia Noller. *Adult Attachment* (Sage Series on Close Relationships). Beverly Hills, CA: Sage Publications, 1996.

Flavell, John H. *The Developmental Psychology of Jean Piaget*. London: Van Nostrand, 1963.

Fukuyama, Francis. *The End of History and the Last Man*. New York, NY: Free Press, 1992.

Galbraith, John Kenneth. *The Culture of Contentment*. Boston, MA: Houghton Mifflin, 1993.

Gallager, Robert G. *Information Theory and Reliable Communication*. New York, NY: John Wiley & Sons, 1968.

Garner, Wendall R. *Uncertainty and Structure as Psychological Concepts*. London and New York, NY: John Wiley & Sons, 1962.

Garratt, Bob. *The Learning Organization: And the Need for Directors Who Think*. Billings, Worcester: Ashgate Publishing Company, 1987.

Gatlin, Lila L. *Information Theory and the Living System*. New York, NY: Columbia University Press, 1972.

Gleick, James. *Chaos: Making a New Science*. New York, NY: Viking Press, 1987.

Globus, Gordon G., Grover Maxwell, and Irwin Savodnik (eds.). *Consciousness and the Brain*. New York, NY: Plenum Press, 1976.

Goerner, Sally J. *Chaos and the Evolving Ecological Universe*. Newark, NJ: Gordon and Breach Publishers, 1994.

Goertzel, Ben. *The Evolving Mind* (The World Futures General Evolution Studies, vol. 6). Newark, NJ: Gordon and Breach Publishers, 1993.

Grossberg, Stephen. *Studies of Mind and Brain: Neural Principles of Learning, Perception, Development, Cognition, and Motor Control*. Dordrecht: D. Reidel Publishing Company, 1982.

Grossberg, Stephen, and Gail A. Carpenter. *Trends in Neurosciences*, 1993, 16(4), pp. 131–137.

Grossberg, Stephen, and Gail A. Carpenter (eds.). *Pattern Recognition by Self-Organizing Neural Networks*. Cambridge, MA: MIT Press, 1991.

Hamel, Gary, and C. K. Prahalad. *Competing for the Future*. Boston, MA: Harvard Business School Press, 1994.

Hammer, Michael, and James Champy. *Reengineering the Corporation*. London: Nicholas Brealey, 1993.

Hampden-Turner, Charles. *Maps of the Mind*. New York, NY: MacMillan Publishing Company, 1982.

Handy, Charles. *The Empty Raincoat*. London: Random House, 1994.

Harlow, H. F., and M. K. Harlow. "Effects of various mother-infant relationships on rhesus monkey behaviors." In: C. Stendler Lavatelli and F. Stendler (eds.), *Readings in Child Behavior and Development*. New York, NY: Harcourt Brace Jovanovitch, 1972.

Harris, Phillip R., and Robert T. Moran. *Managing Cultural Differences*. Houston, TX: Gulf Publishing Company, 1991.

Hersey, Paul, and Ken Blanchard. *Management of Organizational Behavior: Utilizing Human Resources*. Englewood Cliffs, NJ: Prentice-Hall Inc., 1988.

Hinde, Robert A. *Biological Bases of Human Social Behaviour*. London and New York, NY: McGraw-Hill, 1974.

Hinde, Robert A. "The use of differences and similarities in comparative psychopathology." In: G. Serban and A. Kling (eds.), *Animal Models in Human Psychobiology*. London and New York, NY: Plenum Press, 1976.

Hoebeke, Luc. *Making Work Systems Better: A Practitioner's Reflections*. Chichester: John Wiley & Sons, 1994.

Hofstadter, Douglas R. *Gödel, Escher, Bach: An Eternal Golden Braid*. New York, NY: Basic Books, 1979.

Hofstede, Geert. *Culture's Consequences: International Differences in Work-related Values*. Beverly Hills: Sage Publications, Beverly Hills, 1980.

Hofstede, Geert. *Cultures and Organizations: Software of the Mind*. New York, NY: McGraw-Hill, 1991.

Hopstaken, B. A. A., and A. Kranendonk. *Informatieplanning in tweevoud*. Leiden: Stenfert Kroese, 1989.

Hostetler, John Andrew, and Gertrude Enders Huntington. *Children in Amish Society: Socialization and Community Education* (Case Studies in Education and Culture). New York, NY: Holt, Rinehart and Winston, 1971.

Huxley, J., A. C. Hardy, and E. Fords (eds.). *Evolution as a Process*. London: George Allen and Unwin, 1954.

Huxley, Julian Sorell. *Evolution: The Modern Synthesis*. New York, NY: Harper, 1942.

Huxley, Julian Sorell. *Evolution and Ethics*. London: The Pilot Press, 1947.

Huxley, Julian Sorell. *Evolution in Action*. New York, NY: The New American Library, 1957.

Jantsch, Erich. *Design for Evolution: Self-Organization and Planning in the Life of Human Systems*. New York, NY: George Braziller Inc., 1975.

Jantsch, Erich. *The Self-Organizing Universe: Scientific and Human Implications of the Emerg-ing Paradigm of Evolution*. Oxford: Pergamon Press, 1980.

Jantsch, Erich, and C. H. Waddington. *Evolution and Consciousness: Human Systems in Transition*. Reading, MA: Addison-Wesley, 1976.

Jeffrey, Richard C. *Formal Logic: Its Scope and Limits*. New York, NY: McGraw-Hill, 1967.

Jones, Ernest. *The Life and Work of Sigmund Freud. Vol. 1: The Formative Years and the Great Discoveries*. New York, NY: Basic Books, 1953, 1981a.

Jones, Ernest. *The Life and Work of Sigmund Freud. Vol. 2: Years of Maturity*. New York, NY: Basic Books, 1953, 1981b.

Jones, Ernest. *The Life and Work of Sigmund Freud. Vol. 3: The Last Phase, 1919–1939*. New York, NY: Basic Books, 1953, 1981c.

Kaplan, R. D. "The coming anarchy," *Atlantic Monthly*, August, 1996.

Karen, Robert. *Becoming Attached: First Relationships and How They Shape Our Capacity to Love*. Oxford: Oxford University Press, 1998.

Katz, Michael S., and Jeffrey Rothfeder. "Crossing the digital divide…From pricing to channel management to corporate culture, the old economy can teach the new economy a trick or two," *Strategy & Business*, First quarter 2000, pp. 26–41.

Kets de Vries, Manfred F. R. *Organizational Paradoxes: Clinical Approaches to Management*. London and New York, NY: Routledge, 1994.

Kets de Vries, Manfred F. R., and Danny Miller. *The Neurotic Organization: Diagnosing and Changing Counterproductive Styles of Management*. San Francisco, CA: Jossey-Bass, 1984.

Kets de Vries, Manfred F. R., and Danny Miller. *Unstable at the Top: Inside the Troubled Organization*. New York, NY: New American Library, 1988.

Kilmann, Ralph H., Mary J. Saxton, Roy Serpa et al. *Gaining Control of the Corporate Culture*. San Francisco: Jossey-Bass Inc., 1985.

Kotter, John P. *The General Managers*. New York, NY: The Free Press, 1982.

Kotter, John P. *John P. Kotter on What Leaders Really Do* (The Harvard Business Review Book Series). Boston, MA: Harvard Business School Press, 1999.

Kuhn, Thomas S. *The Structure of Scientific Revolutions*. Chicago, IL: University of Chicago Press, 1962.

Lammers, E. "Werknemers Unilever door databestand beter weerbaar," *Trouw*, December 11, 1993.

Larkin, R. J. *Communicating Change: Winning Employee Support for New Business Goals*. New York, NY: McGraw-Hill, 1994.

Laszlo, Ervin. *The Systems View of the World*. New York, NY: George Braziller, 1972.

Laszlo, Ervin (ed.). *The Relevance of General Systems Theory: Papers Presented to Ludwig von Bertalanffy on His Seventieth Birthday*. New York, NY: George Braziller, 1972.

Laszlo, Ervin (ed.). *The World System: Models, Norms, Applications*. New York, NY: George Braziller, 1973.

Laszlo, Ervin (ed.). *The New Evolutionary Paradigm*. Newark, NJ: Gordon and Breach Publishers, 1991.

Laszlo, Ervin (ed.). *The Evolution of Cognitive Maps: New Paradigms for the 21st Century*. Newark, NJ: Gordon and Breach Publishers, 1993.

Laszlo, Ervin. *Vision 2020: Reordering Chaos for Global Survival*. Newark, NJ: Gordon and Breach Publishers, 1994.

Leavitt, David. *The Lost Language of Cranes*. Boston, MA: Mariner Books, 1997.

Levy, A., and U. Merry. *Organizational Transformation, Approaches, Strategies, Theories*. New York, NY: Praeger, 1986.

Lorenz, Konrad. *On Aggression*. New York, NY: Harcourt Brace Jovanovich, 1963.

Lorenz, Konrad. *The Foundations of Ethology*. New York, NY: Touchstone Books, 1981.

Lovejoy, C. O. "The origin of man," *Science*, 1981, 211, pp. 341–350.

Lurija, Aleksandr Romanovich. *The Working Brain: An Introduction to Neuropsychology*. Harmondsworth: Penguin, 1973.

Lynch, G. *Synapses, Circuits, and the Beginnings of Memory* (Cognitive Neuroscience Institute Monograph Series). Cambridge, MA: MIT Press, 1986.

MacKay, Donald M. *Information, Mechanism and Meaning*. Cambridge, MA: MIT Press, 1969.

Maslow, Abraham H. "A theory of human motivation," *Psychological Review*, 1943, 50, pp. 370–396.

Maslow, Abraham H. *Towards a Psychology of Being*. New York, NY: Van Nostrand, 1968.

Maslow, Abraham H. *Motivation and Personality*. New York, NY: Harper & Row, 1970.

Maslow, Abraham H. (Richard J. Lowry and B. G. Maslow, eds.). *The Journals of A. H. Maslow*. Vols. 1 and 2. Monterey, CA: Brooks/Cole Publishing Company, 1979.

Masuli, Ignazio. *Nature and History: The Evolutionary Approach for Social Scientists*. Newark, NJ: Gordon and Breach Publishers, 1990.

McClelland, James L., David E. Rumelhart, and the PDP Research Group. *Parallel Distributed Processing: Explorations in the Microstructures of Cognition. Vol. 2: Psychological and Biological models*. (Vol. 1, see David E. Rumelhart.) Cambridge, MA: MIT Press, 1986.

McKinney, William T., and William E. Bunney. "Animal model of depression," *Arch. Gen. Psychiatry*, 1969, 21, pp. 240–248.

Mills, D. Quinn. *Rebirth of the Corporation*. New York, NY: John Wiley & Sons, 1991.

Minsky, Marvin L. (ed.). *Semantic Information Processing*. Cambridge, MA: MIT Press, 1968.

Mintzberg, Henry. *The Nature of Managerial Work*. New York, NY: Harper & Row, 1973.

Mintzberg, Henry. *The Structuring of Organizations*. Englewood Cliffs, NJ: Prentice-Hall, 1979.

Mintzberg, Henry. "Strategy formation: Schools of thought." In: J. W. Fredrickson (ed.), *Perspectives on Strategic Management*. Boston, MA: Ballinger, 1990.

Mittelstaedt, H. "Discussion, experience and capacity." In: Daniel Porter Kimble (ed.), *The New York Academy of Sciences, New York, Interdisciplinary Communications Program*, 1968, pp. 46–49.

Modis, Theodore. *Conquering Uncertainty: Understanding Corporate Cycles and Positioning Your Company to Survive the Changing Environment* (Business Week Books). New York: McGraw-Hill, 1998.

Monod, Jacques. *Chance and Necessity*. New York, NY: Knopf, 1971.

Morgan, Gareth. "Cybernetics and organization theory: Epistemology or technique?" *Human Relations*, 1982, 35, pp. 521–538.

Morgan, Gareth. "Rethinking corporate strategy: A cybernetic perspective," *Human Relations*, 1983, 36, pp. 345–360.

Morgan, Gareth. *Images of Organization*. Beverly Hills, CA: Sage Publications, 1986.

Moss Kanter, Rosabeth. *When Giants Learn to Dance*. London and New York, NY: Simon & Schuster, 1989.

Moss Kanter, Rosabeth. *The Change Masters*. London: Unwin Hyman, 1983.

Nadler, David A. *Feedback and Organization Development: Using Data-based Methods*. Reading, MA: Addison-Wesley, 1977.

Nagel, Ernest. *The Structure of Science*. New York, NY: Harcourt, Brace and World, 1961.

Nagel, Ernest, and J. R. Newman. *Gödel's Proof*. New York, NY: New York University Press, 1958.

Nicholson, Nigel. "How hardwired is human behavior?" *Harvard Business Review*, July–August 1998.

Nolan, Richard L., and David C. Croson. *Creative Destruction: A Six-Stage Process for Transforming the Organization*. Boston, MA: Harvard Business School Press, 1995.

O'Connor, Joseph, and Ian McDermott. *The Art of Systems Thinking: Essential Skills for Creativity and Problem Solving*. London: Thorsons, 1997.

Ohmae, Kenichi. *The Mind of the Strategist*. Harmondsworth, Middlesex: Penguin Books, 1982.

Parkes, Colin Murray (ed.). *Attachment across the Life Cycle*. London and New York, NY: Routledge, 1991.

Pascale, Richard T. *Managing on the Edge: How the Smartest Companies Use Conflict to Stay Ahead*. New York, NY: Simon & Schuster, 1990.

Pattee, Howard Hunt (ed.). *Hierarchy Theory: The Challenge of Complex Systems*. New York, NY: George Braziller, 1973.

Peters, Thomas J. *Liberation Management: Necessary Disorganization for the Nanosecond Nineties*. New York, NY: Alfred A. Knopf, 1992.

Peters, Thomas J., and Robert H. Waterman Jr. *In Search of Excellence: Lessons from America's Best-Run Companies*. New York, NY: Warner Books, 1982.

Piaget, Jean. *The Psychology of Intelligence*. London: Routledge & Kegan Paul, 1950; New York, NY: Harcourt Brace, 1950.

Piaget, Jean. *The Construction of Reality in the Child*. New York: Basic Books, 1954. (British edition: The Child's Construction of Reality. London: Routledge & Kegan Paul, 1955.)

Piaget, Jean, and Barbel Inhelder. *The Child's Conception of Space*. London: Routledge & Kegan Paul, 1956; New York, NY: Humanities Press, 1956.

Polsky, R., and M. T. McGuire. "An ethological analysis of manic-depressive disorder," *Journal of Nervous and Mental Disease*, 1979, 167, pp. 56–65.

Popper, Karl R., and John C. Eccles. *The Self and Its Brain*. Berlin: Springer-Verlag, 1977.

Pribram, Karl H. *Languages of the Brain: Experimental Paradoxes and Principles in Neuropsychology*. Englewood Cliffs, NJ: Prentice-Hall, 1971.

Pribram, Karl H. Review of *Chance and Necessity* by Jacques Monod, *Perspectives in Biology and Medicine*, 1972.

Pribram, Karl H., and Merton Max Gill. *Freud's Project Re-Assessed: Preface to Contemporary Cognitive Theory and Neuropsychology*. New York, NY: Basic Books, 1976.

Pribram, Karl H. "The frontal cortex: A Luria/Pribram rapprochement." In: E. Goldberg (ed.), *Contemporary Neuropsychology and the Legacy of Luria*. Hillsdale, NJ: Lawrence Erlbaum Associates, 1990.

Pribram, Karl H. *Brain and Perception: Holonomy and Structure in Figural Processing* (John M. MacEachran Lectures Series). Hillsdale, NJ: Lawrence Erlbaum Associates, 1991.

Prigogine, Ilya. *Order Out of Chaos: Man's New Dialogue with Nature*. New York, NY: Random House, 1984.

Quin, Robert E. *Beyond Rational Management: Mastering the Paradoxes and Competing Demands of High Performance*. San Francisco, CA: Jossey-Bass, 1988.

Raelin, Joseph A. *The Clash of Cultures: Managers Managing Professionals*. Boston, MA: Harvard Business School Press, 1991.

Richer, J. "Human ethology and psychiatry." In: H. van Praag (ed.), *Handbook of Biological Psychiatry. Part 1: Disciplines Relevant to Biological Psychiatry*. New York, NY: Marcel Dekker, 1979.

Robertson, J., and J. Robertson. "Young children in brief separation: A fresh look," *Psychoanalytic Study of the Child*, 1972, 26, 264–315.

Rumelhart, David E., James L. McClelland, and the PDP Research Group. *Parallel Distributed Processing, Explorations in the Microstructures of Cognition. Vol. 1: Foundations*. (Vol. 2, see McClelland, James L.) Cambridge, MA: MIT Press, 1986.

Russell, Bertrand. *History of Western Philosophy, and Its Connection with Political and Social Circumstances from the Earliest Times to the Present Day*. London: Allen & Unwin Ltd., 1948.

Russell, Peter. *The White Hole in Time: Our Future Evolution and the Meaning of Now*. San Francisco: Harper, 1992.

Sagan, Carl. *The Dragons of Eden: Speculations on the Evolution of Human Intelligence*. New York, NY: Ballantine Books, 1977.

Schein, Edgar A. *Organizational Culture and Leadership*. San Francisco, CA: Jossey-Bass, 1986.

Schiff, J. L. *Cathexis Reader: Transactional Analysis Treatment of Psychosis*. New York: Harper & Row, 1975.

Schrödinger, Erwin. "Mind and matter." In: *What Is Life? The Physical Aspect of the Living Cell, & Mind and Matter*. Cambridge: Cambridge University Press, 1967.

Semler, Ricardo. *Turning the Tables*. New York, NY: Random House Business Books, 1993.

Senge, Peter M. *The Fifth Discipline: The Art and Practice of the Learning Organization*. New York, NY: Doubleday, 1990.

Shannon, Claude E. "A mathematical theory of information," *Bell System Technical Journal*, 1948, 27, pp. 379–423, 623–656.

Shannon, Claude E., and Warren Weaver. *The Mathematical Theory of Communication*. Urbana: University of Illinois, 1949.

Shay, J. P., and F. T. Rothaermel, "Dynamic competitive strategy: Towards a multi-perspective conceptual framework," *Long Range Planning*, 1999, 32(6), pp. 559–572.

Spitz, R. A., and K. M. Wolf. "Anaclitic depression," *Psychoanalytic Study of the Child* 1946, 26, pp. 264–315.

Spitzer, R. L. (chair). *Workgroup to Revise DSM-III: Diagnostic and Statistical Manual of Mental Disorders*. Washington, DC: American Psychiatric Association, 3rd ed., 1987.

Stacey, Ralph D. *Managing Chaos: Dynamic Business Strategies in an Unpredictable World*. London: Kogan Page, 1992.

Stacey, Ralph D. *The Chaos Frontier: Creative Strategic Control for Business*. London: Butterworth-Heinemann, 1993.

Steinbrunner, John D. *The Cybernetic Theory of Decision: New Dimensions of Political Analysis*. Princeton, NJ: Princeton University Press, 1974.

Sutherland, John W. *A General Systems Philosophy for the Social and Behavioral Sciences*. New York, NY: George Braziller, 1973.

Tichy, Noel M., and D. O. Ulrich. "The leadership challenge: A call for the transformational leader," *Sloan Management Review*, Fall 1984, pp. 59–68.

Tichy, Noel M., and Mary Anne Devanna. *The Transformational Leader: The Key to Global Competitiveness*. New York, NY: John Wiley & Sons, 1986.

Tinbergen, Nikolaas. *The Study of Instinct*. London: Oxford University Press, 1951.

Tinbergen, Nikolaas. *Curious Naturalists*. London: Hamlyn, 1958.

Tinbergen, Nikolaas. "Ethology en Stressziekten," Nobelvoordracht, Vakblad Biologie, 1973, 54, pp. 156–164.

Toffler, Alvin. *Future Shock*. New York, NY: Bantam Books, 1970.

Toffler, Alvin. *The Third Wave*. New York, NY: Bantam Books, 1980.

Toffler, Alvin. *Previews and Premises*. London: Pan Books, 1984.

Toffler, Alvin. *The Adaptive Corporation*. New York, NY: McGraw-Hill, 1985.

Trompenaars, Fons. *Riding the Waves of Culture: Understanding Cultural Diversity in Business*. London: Nicholas Brealey, 1993.

Van Dijk, T. "Wereldwijd Digitaal, de onstuitbare opmars van Internet," *Elsevier*, January 22, 1994.

Van der Erve, Marc. *Evolution Management: Winning Tomorrow's Marketplace*. Oxford and Boston, MA: Butterworth-Heinemann, 1994.

Van der Erve, Marc. *Resonant Corporations: Achieving Growth in Business*. New York, NY: McGraw-Hill, 1998.

Van der Hoog, P. H. "After the organization: Sketches and blueprints for tomorrow's non-organization: Organizational development at AT&T." WCND Utrecht, MBA management project, University of Bradford, 1995.

Van Hasselt, H. R., and F. E. Pels Rijcken. *Bedrijfscultuur, een verkenning in de cultuurkunde van organisaties*. Soest: Employment Services, 1986.

Van Heerden, J. *De zorgelijke staat van het onbewuste*. Meppel: Boom, 1982.

Van Heijenoort, J. *From Frege to Gödel: A Source Book in Mathematical Logic*. Cambridge, MA: Harvard University Press, 1977.

Van IJzendoorn, M. H. *Opvoeden in geborgenheid: een kritische analyse van Bowlby's attachmenttheorie*. Van Deventer: Van Loghum Slaterus, 1982.

Van Lawick-Goodall, Jane van. "Some aspects of mother-infant relationships in a group of wild chimpanzees." In: H. R. Schaffer (ed.), *The Origin of Human Social Relations*. New York, NY: Academic Press, 1971.

Von Bertalanffy, Ludwig. "The theory of open systems in physics and biology," *Science*, 1950, 3, pp. 23–29.

Von Bertalanffy, Ludwig. *Robots, Men and Minds: Psychology in the Modern World*. New York, NY: George Braziller, 1967.

Von Bertalanffy, Ludwig. *General Systems Theory: Foundations, Development, Applications*. New York, NY: George Braziller, 1968.

Von Bertalanffy, Ludwig. *Das Biologische Weltbild*. Berlin: Francke, 1965.

Von Foerester, Heinz, and G. W. Zopf. *Principles of Self-Organization*. New York: Pergamon Press, 1962.

Vuyk, R. "Enkele aspecten van Bowlby's attachment theory in het licht van recente ontwikkelingen in de ethology en de psychologie," in *Kind en Adolescent*, jrg. 4, 1983, nr. 1, pp. 2–22.

Watzlawick, Paul. *How Real Is "Real"? Communication, Disinformation, Confusion*. New York: Random House, 1977.

Watzlawick, Paul, John H. Weakland, and Richard Fisch. *Change: Principles of Problem Formation and Problem Resolution*. New York, NY: W. W. Norton & Company, 1988.

Wiener, Norbert. *Cybernetics: Or Control and Communication in the Animal and the Machine*. Cambridge, MA: MIT Press, 1961.

Wiener, Norbert. *Ex-prodigy: My Childhood and Youth*. Cambridge, MA: MIT Press, 1964.

Wiener, Norbert. *God & Golem, Inc.: A Comment on Certain Points Where Cybernetics Impinges on Religion*. Cambridge, MA: MIT Press, 1964.

Wiener, Norbert (Masani, P., ed.). *Norbert Wiener: Collected Works. Vol. 4: Cybernetics, Science and Society; Ethics, Aesthetics and Literary Criticism; Book Reviews & Obituaries* (Mathematicians of Our Times Series). Cambridge, MA: MIT Press, 1985.

Wiener, Norbert. *The Human Use of Human Beings: Cybernetics & Society*. Philadelphia, PA: Da Capo Press, 1988.

Wilde, L. de. "Een ethologische visie op depressie," *Tijdschrift voor Psychiatrie*, 1983, 25(9), pp. 611–622.

Wilson, Edward O. *In Search of Nature*. Washington DC: Island Press, 1996.

Zaleznik, Abraham. *Power and the Corporate Mind*. Chicago, IL: Bonus Books, 1985.

Zaleznik, Abraham, and Manfred F. R. Kets de Vries. *Power and the Corporate Mind: How to Use Rather Than Misuse Leadership*. Boston, MA: Houghton Mifflin, 1975.

Zukav, Gary. *The Dancing Wu Li Masters: An Overview of the New Physics*. New York, NY: Bantam Books, 1979.

Zwart, Cees. *Gericht veranderen van organisaties: beheerste ontwikkeling als permanente activiteit*. Rotterdam: Lemniscaat, 1972.